Walking the Camino de Santiago

Robert Hamilton

www.spanishsteps.eu

Walking the Camino de Santiago, 1st Edition

Cover photo: Lunchtime for Damien & Joe between Roncesvalles & Larrasoaña
Back cover photo: Santiago de Compostela Cathedral

I have done my utmost to ensure that all the information in this guide is as accurate as possible, but I cannot accept any responsibility for any loss, injury or inconvenience experienced by any person using this book.

If you find new accommodation along the way please let us know about it by emailing Robert at the address below or posting it on our Facebook page and we will update the site & book for other pilgrims.

Some of the profits from the sale of this book will go to the Brain Research Trust: www.brt.org.uk

Please take a few minutes to leave a positive review for this book on Amazon.

Thank you.

Web: www.spanishsteps.eu

Facebook: www.facebook.com/walkthecaminodesantiago

Twitter: www.twitter.com/_spanish_steps

Email: robert@spanishsteps.eu

Contents

Camino History

In Brief

The Way of St James has existed for over a thousand years. It was one of the most important Christian pilgrimages during mediaeval times. Saint James was beheaded in Jerusalem in AD44 on the orders of King Herod Agrippa. The body of the first apostle to be martyred was carried in a stone boat to the coast of **Galicia**.

He was then buried in **Santiago de Compostela** where he lay forgotten for many centuries. According to legend a star led a shepherd, Pelayo, from Galicia to the grave in 813AD. The Bishop of nearby **Iria Flavia** confirmed the discovery.

King of Asturias & León Alfonso II ordered that the cathedral be built in honour of Saint James on the site of his grave.

The revival of the story of Saint James came at the start of the Reconquista of Christianity in Spain. During this period it is said that Saint James appeared on horseback and helped fight against the Moors.

His most famous appearance happened at the battle of **Clavijo** in 844 where he single handedly slaughtered thousands of Moors. This is where the images of **Santiago Matamoros**, Saint James the Moor Slayer, on horseback originate. Soon after, Saint James became the patron saint of Spain and Santiago de Compostela quickly became the third largest pilgrimage destination next to **Rome** and **Jerusalem**.

The Way can take one of any number of pilgrimage routes to **Santiago de Compostela**.

Traditionally, as with most pilgrimages, the Way of Saint James began at one's home and ended at the pilgrimage site.

However a few of the routes are considered main ones,

particularly the **Camino Francés**. During the Middle Ages, the route was very popular. However, the Black Plague, the Protestant Reformation and political unrest in 16th- century Europe resulted in its decline.

By the 1980s, only a few pilgrims arrived in **Santiago** annually. However, since then, the route has attracted a growing number of modern-day pilgrims from around the globe. The Council of Europe declared the route the first European Cultural Route in

October 1987; it was also named one of UNESCO's World Heritage Sites.

Pre-Christian History of the Camino

Pagan symbols have been claimed to exist along the route. Some pilgrims are more attracted to the pagan legends popularly attributed to the walk, than to the Christian history.

One legend is that walking the route was a pagan fertility ritual; this however is based on the explanation of scallop shell being a symbol of the pilgrimage.

An alternative interpretation is that the scallop, which resembles the setting sun, was the focus of pre-Christian Celtic rituals of the area.

There are also claims that the pre-Christian origin of the Way of St. James was a Celtic death journey, westwards towards the setting sun, terminating at the End of the World (Finisterra) on the "Coast of Death" (Costa da

Morte) and the "Sea of Darkness" (that is, the Abyss of Death, the Mare Tenebrosum,

Latin for the Atlantic Ocean, itself named after the Dying Civilization of Atlantis).

The Camino During the Mediaeval Period

The earliest records of visits paid to the shrine dedicated to St. James at **Santiago de Compostela** date from the 8th century, in the time of the Kingdom of Asturias.

The pilgrimage to the shrine became the most renowned mediaeval pilgrimage, and it became customary for those who returned from **Compostela** to carry back with them a Galician scallop shell as proof of their completion of the journey.

This practice was gradually extended to other pilgrimages. The earliest recorded pilgrims from beyond the **Pyrenees** visited the shrine in the middle of the 10th century, but it seems

that it was not until a century later that large numbers of pilgrims from abroad started making the journey. The earliest records of pilgrims that arrived from England belong to the period between 1092 and 1105.

However, by the early 12th century the pilgrimage had become a highly organized affair. One of the great proponents of the pilgrimage in the 12th century was Calixtus II who started the Compostelan Holy Years.

The official guide in those times was the Codex Calixtinus. Published around 1140, the 5th book of the Codex is still considered the definitive source for many modern guidebooks.

Four pilgrimage routes listed in the Codex originate in France and converge at Puente la Reina. From there, a well-defined route crosses northern Spain, linking **Burgos**, **Carrión** de los Condes, Sahagún, León, Astorga, and Santiago de Compostela.

In 1189 Pope Alexander II declared Santiago de Compostela a Holy City.

He then declared that any pilgrim completing the Camino during Holy Year would not have to endure purgatory in the afterlife and those who completed the pilgrimage during any other year would only have to do half the normal time.

It was the norm during this time for criminals to be sentenced to walk the Camino as punishment. Although many convicts, if they had the money, would pay someone else to complete it for them.

Due to the huge numbers who made their way to Santiago, lots of towns and cities began to appear along the way. Churches and a series of hospitals and hospices were built to provide for the daily needs of pilgrims on their way to, and from, Compostela. These had royal protection and were a lucrative source of revenue. A new genre of ecclesiastical architecture, Romanesque, with its massive archways, was designed to cope with huge devout crowds. There was also the now- familiar paraphernalia of tourism, such as the selling of badges and souvenirs. Since the Christian symbol for James the Greater was the scallop shell, many pilgrims would wear this as a sign to anyone on the road that they were a pilgrim.

This gave them privileges to sleep in churches and ask for free meals, but also warded off thieves who did not dare attack devoted pilgrims.

Pilgrims would walk the Way of St. James in order to arrive at the great cathedral in the main square of Compostela to pay homage to St. James. So many pilgrims have laid their hands on the pillar just inside the doorway of the church that a groove has been worn in the stone.

The Modern Day Camino

The popularity of the Camino faded until a revival began in the 1960s thanks to the efforts of people like **O'Cebreiro**'s parish priest, **Don Elias Valiña Sampedro**, who wrote a guide on the Camino and traveled around Europe giving lectures on the subject.

Today thousands of Christian pilgrims and other travelers set out each year from their front doorstep, or from popular starting points across Europe, to make their way to **Santiago de Compostela**.

Most make the journey on foot, some travel on bicycle, and a few hardened travelers go on horseback or by donkey.

In addition to people undertaking a religious pilgrimage, there are many travelers and hikers who walk the route for non-religious reasons: travel, sport, or simply the challenge of weeks of walking in a foreign land.

Also, many consider the experience a spiritual adventure to remove them from the bustle of modern life. It acts as a retreat for many modern "pilgrims".

Routes to Santiago

Pilgrims on the **Way of St. James** walk for weeks or months to visit the city of **Santiago de Compostela**. They can follow many routes but the most popular route is the **French Way**, **Camino Francés**.

The most common starting points are **Saint-Jean-Pied-de-Port** or **Somport** on the French side of the Pyrenees or **Roncesvalles** on the Spanish side.

However, many pilgrims begin further afield, in one of the four French towns that are common and traditional starting points: **Le Puy**, **Vézelay**, **Arles** and **Tours**. **Cluny**, site of the celebrated medieval abbey, was another important rallying point for pilgrims, and, in 2002, it was integrated into the official European pilgrimage route linking **Vézelay** and **Le Puy**.

The **Via de la Plata**, *The Silver Way*, is another popular route, and is 1000km long. It is much less frequented than the **French Way** or even the **Northern Way** but in recent years it has gained popularity amongst pilgrims from around the world. The **Via de La Plata** starts in **Seville** from where it goes north to **Zamora** via **Cáceres** and **Salamanca**.

After **Zamora** there are two options. The first route heads west and reaches **Santiago** via **Ourense**. The other route continues north to **Astorga** from where pilgrims can continue west along the **Camino Francés** to **Santiago**.

Another popular route is the **Camino Portugués**, **Portuguese Way**, which begins at **Porto** in northwest **Portugal**.

Pilgrims travel north crossing the **Lima** and **Minho** rivers before entering Spain and then on to **Padron** before arriving **at Santiago**.

It is the second most important way, after the French one and is 227 km long.

A popular starting point for a 108 km walk to **Santiago** is at **Valença**, **Portugal**, by the Spanish border, through **Tui** in the province of **Galicia**

Getting There & Back
Traveling from the UK & Ireland

The handiest way to get to **St Jean Pied de Port** is to get a flight **to Biarritz**. **Ryanair** offer direct flights **from Birmingham**, **London** (Stansted) and **Dublin**.

Easyjet also offer flights from **London** (Gatwick) **and Bristol**.

British Airways fly to **Madrid** from **London** and onto a number of destinations in the north of Spain

From **Biarritz** you can take the bus to **Bayonne** and connecting train to **St Jean Pied de Port**. Another option would be to take a taxi to **St Jean** at a cost of around €100.

You could consider sharing the costs with other pilgrims if there i s any heading your way. You could also consider flying to **Bilbao** from **London** (Stansted) or From **Dublin** with **Aer Lingus**.

From here you can take a bus or train to **Bayonne**, **Roncesvalles**, **Pamplona** or **Burgos**. Depending on where you want to start your walk from.

You might also consider flying to **Madrid, Valladolid (Ryanair** from London Stansted) if you are starting near **Burgos** and **Santander (Ryanair** from **Dublin** or **London** Stansted) if you are starting near **León**.

Traveling from within Europe

There are lots of European budget airlines that fly to all the major cities along the Camino or check out the following websites:

www.expedia.com

www.britishairways.com

www.vueling.com

www.clickair.com

www.airberlin.com

www.iberia.com

www.aerlingus.com

If you are planning to start in **St Jean Pied de Port** take a flight to **Paris** and then get a train to **Bayonne** and then get a connecting train to **St Jean**.

There are lots of cheap bus and rail connections throughout Europe, which will take you to or close to any of the main points along the Camino.

Check out the following:

www.eurolines.co.uk

www.renfe.es/horarios

Traveling from outside Europe

This depends on where you decide to start your walk.

If you plan on starting in **St Jean Pied de Port** then you are best getting a flight to **Paris** or **Biarritz**.

Ryanair fly to **Biarritz** from **Dublin** & **London**.

American Airlines travel from all the major cities in **America** to **Paris**.

If you are traveling from Canada plan your travels with **Air France Canada** one of the leading Canadian airlines, which fly from **Montreal** and **Toronto** to many European destinations.

If you fly to **Paris** you can then get a train to **Bayonne** and then get a connecting train to **St Jean**.

If you fly to **Biarritz**, on arrival take the airport bus to **Bayonne** and then get a connecting train to **St Jean**.

Walking Equipment

The best advice that we can give you is to bring as little as possible. Every year we have travelled on the Camino we aim for **8kg - 10kg** of gear in our backpack.

The maximum size of your backpack should be 50 litres, and remember there is no need to fill it. If you plan to carry a little food, for your daily journey, and some water this will bring the weight of your backpack up to around 10kg, which should be your max.

Remember that there are many towns and villages along the way where you can buy whatever it is you may need.

Try to ensure that whatever weight you are carrying is evenly spread in your backpack and make sure the straps are tight enough so that you are carrying most of this weight on your hips and not on your shoulders.

Footwear should be considered the most important thing you will need for the trip. A lot of people will advise you on buying a pair really good boots but we have found that a good pair of walking shoes will do a better job.

They are lighter on the feet and more comfortable, particularly on hot days, and leave you less prone to blisters. We would also advise you to take a pair of sandals or running shoes with you for walking around in the evenings.

Some essentials:

* Rucksack (Between 50 - 65 litre)
* A pair of decent walking poles. See this article for some advice
* Some rain gear, including a backpack cover and a pac-a-mac or poncho
* Broad brimmed hat
* Sunglasses
* 2 light weight T-shirts (sports tops would be best. They are light weight and quick drying)
* 1 light fleece (It can get chilly in the evenings)
* A pair of walking trousers
* A pair of shorts
* 3 pairs of underwear
* 3 pairs of socks
* Walking Boots or Walking Shoes (We would recommend a good pair of walking shoes).
* Sandals or running shoes for the evenings
* Light sleeping bag
* Sleeping mat
* Some travel detergent
* Platypus Water Carrier
* Sunscreen – two small pouches should be enough
* Toiletries – keep things to a minimum. Remember that there are plenty of shops along the way
* Small First Aid Kit – include Compeed/Second Skin, plasters, and ibuprofen. There are plenty of chemists (farmacias) along the way so only a small amount should do.
* Microfibre travel towel
* Mobile Phone
* Digital Camera
* Earplugs – Bring some spare ones. Lots of heavy snorers out there!! (We recommend these, they're very good)
* Small torch such as a Maglite
* Swiss army knife

* Travel set of cutlery

This is by no means an exhaustive list.

We have found it met our requirements for all the trips we have been on so far.

One more thing to consider is reading materials. A couple of paperbacks should be fine as long as you would be happy to leave them behind for someone else to read when you have finished them.

And you might want to consider keeping a small journal.

Your main aims are to keep your backpack as light as possible (8kg - 10kg) and help make your walk as enjoyable as possible.

http://tinyurl.com/camino-gear

Choosing the Right Footwear

When setting out to walk the **Camino de Santiago**, having the right footwear is essential.

Making the wrong choice in footwear could lead to painful blisters or, worse still, having to call your walk off early due to injury. You'll read lots of information online about what is best to wear when making the track across Spain.

The first thing to take into consideration is the type of terrain you will be covering over the course of your walk.

Most of the **Camino Francés** is along fairly flat tracks through open countryside and sometimes parallel to some roads. There is the occasional exception such as the climb up to **O'Cebreiro**, although there is a path to follow, which can be quite rocky in places.

For this reason I recommend hill walking / trekking boots or shoes which have been designed for year round dry hill walking, such as those made by North Face or Salomon.

This type of footwear will provide adequate support and grip for this type of terrain where paths and trails are encountered a lot.

On my first two trips along the **Camino Francés**, I wore a pair of Salomon walking / trekking shoes and had experienced no blisters or foot problems whatsoever.

Try to make sure your choice of boots or shoes are water proofed with a waterproof liner, as you will probably experience the odd shower along the way, particularly in **Galicia**.

Low-level paths such as those found along the **Camino** can sometimes be slightly uneven with some lose stones or gravel and are not particularly steep.

Walking / trekking boots designed for this type of walking will provide enough support if you intend to carry a reasonably packed rucksack containing around 10kg of gear, which should be ample for a comfortable trip along the **Camino de Santiago**. http://tinyurl.com/camino-footwear

Best Time To Walk The Camino

The best months to walk the Camino are May/June and September/October. Most walkers hit the road early morning so temperatures during these months are perfect for walking. Because of the intense heat it is not recommended to attempt walking during the months of July and August. This coupled with the fact that these months are the most popular for Spanish walkers making finding a bed in the albergues a little more difficult. Whilst walking in the Basque Region and in Galicia you should be prepared for rain all year round.

Walking In Winter

During the winter months from November to October the weather makes the journey across the north of Spain more difficult. This isn't helped by the fact tht a lot of the pilgrim hostels, albergues, are closed.

Walking in the winter will require more time as the days get shorter and the weather conditions deteriorate. Take extra care oin the ore remote areas of the walk as fog and snow can affect visibility and it is all too easy to stray of the designated route. You should also reconsider walking the Route Napoleon from Saint-Jean-Pied-de-Port towards Roncesvalles opting instead for the alternative route along the road. To be on the safe side you should check what accommodation is available bfore starting out each day.

FAQs

How fit do I have to be to walk the Camino de Santiago?

The good news for most of us is, not very.

You will find that after a relatively short period of time your body will get into the routine of walking the road with a rucksack on your back. This really does depend on the weight of your backpack. I can't stress this enough, your backpack, ideally, should not weigh more than 10kg and take into consideration any food and water you may need to carry on the day.

So 9kg would be the ideal weight of your pack when setting out on your walk. You really do not need that much stuff with you, the less the better.

After a few days of getting up and getting on the road to walk 20km - 30km (depending on what you are comfortable with) will very soon get your body into good shape and you will be pleasantly surprised and how good you feel when you arrive at your final destination.

You will definitely return home from walking the Camino de

Santiago feeling much better physically and mentally, although your feet might tell a different story.

Footwear is a very important factor to consider. Do you really need a pair of walking boot? Not really. I have found over the years that a **good pair of walking shoes** will do a better job considering the terrain that you will be covering.

The Camino de Santiago is mainly along dirt tracks, some rockier than others and the weather; again depending on the time of year is usually dry, with the exception of Galicia where it tends to rain more. So I would recommend a good pair of walking shoes with a waterproof lining. So if you are concerned about your level of fitness, don't worry. Just pack up and go for it and on the first few days walk at a reasonable speed and cover a distance that you are comfortable with. And most importantly if you feel any sign of

blisters or problems with your feet, stop immediately and fix the problem.

Will I need to be able to speak Spanish when walking the Camino de Santiago?

For the most part you will be able to get along fine without being able to speak much Spanish. Volunteers, hospitaleros, who can speak a number of languages, maintain most albergues.

I have stayed in albergues where the *hospitalero* has been from France, Holland, Ireland and England.

Most restaurants and bars will understand what you want, although I suppose if you walk in to a restaurant or a bar there is only a few things that you really do want. My father is now fluent in pub Spanish, he very quickly familiarised himself with the Spanish for 'large beer', *'cerveza*

grande' and 'red wine', '*vino tinto*'
Saying that, the Spanish people really do appreciate it if you even try to communicate with them in their own language, no matter how bad your Spanish is.

I have written a Spanish phrasebook, which I have included with this guide.

If you would like to learn a bit more I highly recommend a course by **Michel Thomas**, this course can be loaded onto your iPod / MP3 player and you can learn as you walk the Camino.

I have listened to this course a few times and can honestly say that I learnt more in a few hours than I did over 2 years going to evening classes.

http://tinyurl.com/camino-spanish

How Much Will It Cost?

Walking the Camino de Santiago should take roughly 5 weeks from start to finish. The overall cost should be an average of

€700 for accommodation on pilgrim hostels and food & drink. This does not include travel to and from the Camino.

The Pilgrim Passport

The Pilgrim Passport / *Credencial* is a document issued by the cathedral authorities in **Santiago**, and made available to pilgrims at various points along the routes - e.g. at **St. Jean Pied de Port**, and at some churches and albergues along the way.

To prevent people abusing the hospitality of the pilgrimage, access to the albergues are restricted to those carrying

14

Credencials. You should always try to remember to have your *Credencial* stamped and dated daily with a local stamp / *sello* at whatever albergue you stay at, the local church, town hall, *ayuntamiento*, or the local police station, *Guardia Civil*, to keep a record of your pilgrimage. Each town/albergue has it's own original stamp / sello, some more decorative than others.

On completion of your pilgrimage at **Santiago de Compostela** you can present your *Credencial* at the Pilgrim Office beside the Cathedral. You will then be given your **Compostela Certificate**, the traditional document, in Latin, confirming your completion of the pilgrimage.

It is required that walkers and pilgrims on horseback must have completed at least the last 100km and cyclists the last

200 km in order to qualify for the *Compostela*. A few years ago the Pilgrim Office in **Santiago**

started asking pilgrims who start their Camino in **Galicia** to try and get two stamps per day in their credencials.

So if you're starting from anywhere before **Ponferrada** make sure to get two stamps a day, and get hold of another *Credencial* if you need room for the extra stamps. If you've come from outside **Galicia**, one stamp a day within **Galicia** is enough.

How & Where to get your Credencial / Pilgrim Passport

You can get your *Credencial* from:

Confraternity of St James: www.csj.org.uk

American Pilgrims on the Camino: www.americanpilgrims.com

Confraternity of Saint James Australia: www.csj.org.uk/australia.htm

Canadian Company of Pilgrims: www.santiago.ca

Irish Society of the Friends of St James: www.stjamesirl.com

Confraternity of Saint James of South Africa:
www.csjofsa.za.org

You can also register for your *Credencial* at a number of potential starting points although this is subject to change.

* If you are starting in **le Puy**, go to the Cathedral, or the local association of the **Amis de St Jacques**

* If you are starting in **St Jean Pied-de-Port**, go to Accueil St Jacques, 39 rue de la Citadelle

* If you choose **Roncesvalles** as your starting point then you need to go to the Abbey

If you are starting at any other point in Spain you should go to the local albergue, church, police station or the Town Hall, Ayuntamiento, to register.

You will be required to have your passport with you, as your passport number is required for registration.

Pilgrim Hostals

In Spain and Southern France, pilgrim's hostels can be found along the common routes providing overnight

accommodation for pilgrims who hold a pilgrim passport, *credencial.* In Spain this type of accommodation is called a refugio or an albergue, both of which are similar to youth hostels or hostelries in the French system of Gîtes d'étape.

Beds are usually in dormitories, and they cost between three and seven Euros per night, but a few operate on voluntary donations, especially in Galicia, and are known as *donativos*.

Pilgrims are usually limited to one night's accommodation unless they are carrying an injury or re in need of a rest. The local parish, the local council, private owners, or pilgrims' associations may run these hostels.

Occasionally these albergues are located in monasteries, such as the one in **Samos**, Spain, which is run by monks, as is the one in **Santiago de Compostela**. Most pilgrims carry a pilgrim passport, credencial, which allows overnight accommodation in the albergues.

The *credencial* is stamped with the official St. James stamp, *sello*, of each town or refugio at which the pilgrim has stayed.

It provides pilgrims with a record of where they ate or slept, but also serves as proof to the Pilgrim's office in Santiago that the journey has been completed according to the official route.

The *credencial* is available at albergues, tourist offices, some local parish houses, and outside Spain, through the national St. James organisation of that country.

Confraternities

Confraternity of St James: www.csj.org.uk

American Pilgrims on the Camino: www.americanpilgrims.com

CSJ Australia: www.csj.org.uk/australia.htm

Canadian Company of Pilgrims: www.santiago.ca

Irish Society of the Friends of St James: www.stjamesirl.com

CSJ of South Africa: www.csjofsa.za.org

A lot of the albergues are open all year round with most opening between Easter and October. The list of albergues is constantly growing as the Camino de Santiago grows in popularity.

Albergues are run in a first come first serve basis and although we have included telephone numbers for a lot of the albergues, these are to be used in emergencies only or if you are walking the Camino in winter time and need to check that the albergues are open. Keep in mind that the closer you get to Santiago the busier the route

becomes and finding a bed for the night at your destination can become quite 'competitive'.

Be prepared to leave a little earlier in the morning to arrive in time to find a bed! Most albergues are clean and well looked after, there are of course a few exceptions.

They open at around 13:00 and you are expected to be up and out in the morning before 08:30.

Lots of people start out early in the morning so expect to hear movement and the rustling of plastic bags from as early as 05:30am. If you are a light sleeper, a good set (or two) of earplugs is advisable.

The stamped *Credencial* is also necessary if the pilgrim wants to obtain a *Compostela,* a certificate of completion of the pilgrimage. Most often the stamp can be obtained in the albergue,

Cathedral or local church. If the church is closed, the town hall or office of tourism can provide a stamp, as well as nearby youth hostels or private St. James addresses.

As the pilgrimage approaches **Santiago de Compostela** however, the increased number of pilgrims causes many of the stamps in small towns to be self-service, while in the larger towns there are several options to obtain the necessary stamp.

Pilgrim Certificate

The *Compostela* is a certificate of accomplishment given to

pilgrims on completing the Way. To earn the *Compostela* you need to walk a minimum of 100 km, cyclists must cycle at least 200 km.

For walkers, that would mean a starting point in the small city of **Sarria**, which has good transportation connections via bus and rail to other places in Spain.

Pilgrims arriving in **Santiago de Compostela** who have walked at least the last 100 km, or cycled 200 km are eligible for a *Compostela* from the Pilgrim's Office in **Santiago de Compostela**. The *Compostela* has been customary since the Early Middle Ages

The full text of the certificate is in Latin and reads:

CAPITULUM hujus Almae Apostolicae et Metropolitanae Ecclesiae Compostellanae sigilli Altaris Beati Jacobi Apostoli custos, ut omnibus Fidelibus et Perigrinis ex toto terrarum Orbe,

devotionis affectu vel voti causa, ad limina Apostoli Nostri Hispaniarum Patroni ac Tutelaris **SANCTI JACOBI**

convenientibus, authenticas visitationis litteras expediat, omnibus et singulis praesentes inspecturis, notum facit : (Latin version of your name) Hoc sacratissimum Templum pietatis causa devote visitasse. In quorum fidem praesentes litteras, sigillo ejusdem Sanctae Ecclesiae munitas, ei confero. Datum Compostellae die (day) mensis (month) anno Dni (year). Canonicus Deputatus pro

Peregrinis

Translated into English it reads:

"The Chapter of this Holy Apostolic Metropolitan Cathedral of St. James, custodian of the seal of St. James' Altar, to all faithful and pilgrims who come from everywhere over the world as an act of devotion, under vow or promise to the Apostle's Tomb, our Patron and Protector

of Spain, witnesses in the sight of all who read this document, that: (your name) has visited devoutly this Sacred Church in a religious sense.

Witness whereof I hand this document over to him, authenticated by the seal of this Sacred Church. Given in St. James de Compostela on the (day)......(month)......(year)A.D. ....Chapter Secretary"

The pilgrim passport is examined carefully for stamps and dates. If a key stamp is missing, or if the pilgrim does not claim a religious purpose for their pilgrimage, the compostela may be refused. The Pilgrim office of Santiago awards more than 100,000 compostelas per year to pilgrims from over 100 countries. Pilgrims who receive their Compostela the day before, have their countries of origin and the starting point of their pilgrimage announced at the Mass.

The musical and visual highlight of the mass is the synchronisation of the beautiful 'Hymn to Christ' with the spectacular swinging of the huge '*Butafumeiro*'.

It's also worth nothing that your *Compostela* may be presented at the **Parador Hotel de los Reyes Católicos** who provide 10 free pilgrim meals three times a day. You will have to queue at the garage door, down the ramp to the left.

Camino Francés

Camino Francés, *The French Way*, is by far the most popular of all the routes of the Way of St. James, the ancient pilgrimage route to Santiago de Compostela.

The Camino Francés can be divided into 3 main sections:

• The rolling hills of the Basque country

• The hot, flat central section of the meseta

• The green hills of Galicia.

It runs from **St Jean Pied de Port** on the French side of the Pyrenees to **Roncesvalles** on the Spanish side and then another 780km on to Santiago de Compostela through the major cities of **Pamplona**, **Logroño**, **Burgos** and **Léon**.

The pathway is marked with yellow arrows painted on walls, trees, and buildings all the way to **Santiago**.

Paths from the cities of **Tours**, **Vézelay**, and **Le Puy-en-Velay** meet at **St Jean Pied de Port**. A fourth French route originates in **Arles**, in Provence, and crosses the French-Spanish border at a different point, between the Pyrenees towns of **Somport** and **Canfranc**.

This fourth route follows the Aragonese Way and joins the main **Camino Francés** route at **Puente la Reina**, south of **Pamplona**, in **Navarre**, about seven hundred kilometres **from Santiago de Compostela**.

A typical journey on the **Camino Francés** should take at least a month allowing for one or two rest days along the way. The path itself, with a few exceptions, is usually fairly flat and wide, with a good even surface.

We have documented the **Camino Frances** over 32 stages, starting at **St Jean Pied de Port**, providing you with information as well as accommodation in each town & village along the way. This is just a suggested itinerary; you should feel free to start the Camino wherever you want. Although to qualify for a *Compostela* you have to complete at least 100km if walking or 200km if you are on a bicycle.

It is also worth noting that each day you can walk as much or as little of the route that you feel comfortable with. Due to the numbers of pilgrims walking on the Camino you are permitted to stay in an albergue for one night only unless you are injured or in need of a rest.

The icons displayed for each stage indicate the services and facilities you will find at each stop:

A : Albergues

H : Hotels, Hostals

△ : Camping

🍴 : Restaurants

☕ : Bars

€ : Bank

𝑖 : Tourist Information

🛒 : Shops

✚ : Chemist / Pharmacy

@ : Internet Access

There are plenty of **albergues**, pilgrim hostels, & refugios along the way where you get the opportunity to meet other pilgrims. You will also find a range of more expensive accommodation such as private albergues, pensións and hotels along the way.

I've list as many of these as we can, and if you know of any other albergues, hotels, pensions etc that are not on the list contact me at **robert@spanishsteps.eu** with the details.

St Jean Pied de Port

St. Jean Pied de Port, Saint John at the foot of the mountain pass, is a small picturesque walled town close to **Ostabat** in the French Pyrenean foothills.

The original town at nearby **Saint-Jean-le-Vieux** was razed to the ground in 1177 by the troops of Richard the Lionheart after a siege. The Kings of Navarre refounded the town on its present site shortly afterwards.

The town was once a part of the Spanish province of **Navarra** and the Basque language is still spoken on both sides of the border and they still share similar traditions such as the game of *Pelota*, similar to the Irish game of handball.

The town has traditionally been an important point on the Way of St. James, the pilgrimage to **Santiago de Compostela**, as it stands at the base of the Roncevaux Pass across the Pyrenees. It is the last stopping place where three pilgrims' routes,

Tours, **Le Puy-en-Velay** and **Limoges**, all meet before crossing the Pyrenees into Spain.

In 1998, the **Porte St-Jacques** (city gate) was added to the UNESCO World Heritage Sites as part of the sites along the Routes of **Santiago de Compostela** in France.

The main street is the cobbled **Rue de Citadelle** which runs downhill past the 14th century **Eglise Notre Dame de St Jean Pied de Port** which has a fountain decorated with scallop shells outside and the Porte Notre Dame, the town gate.

Continuing on you will come to a bridge crossing the river Nive.

From the bridge, there are beautiful views of the old houses with balconies overlooking the Nive. Many of the buildings and retain distinctive features, including inscriptions over their doors.

At the top of the Rue de Citadelle you can visit what remains of the 17th Century **Citadel** which has now been converted into a college. The **Prison de Eveques**, *Prison of Bishops*, is on this street as is a small museum dedicated the **Camino de Santiago**.

Pilgrim Passport / Credencial

You can get your pilgrim passport / *credencial* from the pilgrim office Accueill at Rue de Citadelle 39 Tel: (0033) 0559 37 05 09. It is open all day except at lunchtime.

Layout

St Jean Pied de Port is a fairly small town and is quite easy to find your way around. The **Rue de Citadelle** runs through the middle of the town. The Tourist office can be found on the **Place Général de Gaulle** nearby and is open Jul & Aug Mon–Sat 9am–12.30 & 2–7pm; Sep–Jun Mon–Sat 9am–noon & 2–7pm.

Getting There & Back

Book flights to/from **Biarritz, Toulouse**, **Pamplona** or **Bilboa**

You can then take a bus or train to Bayonne and then a bus on to St Jean.

Accommodation

Albergue Municipal, Rue de Citadelle 55.

Beds: 18, Open all year round. Has a kitchen facility.

Albergue Le Chemin Vers L'Etoile, 21, rue d' Espagne. **T:** 0559 37 20 71. **Beds:** 18. Open Feb - Oct. Has cooking & laundry facilities as well as Internet access.

Albergue L'Esprit de Chemin, Rue de Citadelle 40 **Beds:** 18, Open Apr - Sept.

Offers dining services as well as lunch for the next days walk.

Albergue Esponda, Place du Trinquet 5
T: (0033) 0559 50 01 65
Beds: 20, Open all year round. Has a kitchen facility.

Hotel Ramuntcho ** Rue de Citadelle 24.
T: (0033) - 0559 37 35 17
E: hotel.ramuntcho@wanadoo.fr

Hotel de Remparts **,
Place Floquet 16.
T: (0033) 0559 37 13 79

E: remparts.hotel@wanadoo.fr
W: www.touradour.com

Hotel Etche Ona **
Place Floquet 15.
T: (0033) 0559 37 01 14

Hotel De Pyréneés *** Place Général de Gaulle 19.
T: (0033) 0559 37 01 01

W: www.hotel-les-pyrenees.com

Where to Eat

The Basque cuisine is one of the finest cuisines around. Basque specialities include veal stew, ham "piperade", calf's sweetbread, chipirons, cepe omelette , stream trout, confit de canard, sauteed eel and parsley. For dessert try ewe's cheese with black cherry jam, ewe's cottage cheese and the inimitable, gâteau basque sont les délices de notre région.

St Jean Pied de Port specialise in *fromage de brebis or Ossaulraty*, sheeps cheese, local trout and *pipérade*, omelette with peppers & Bayonne ham.

There are plenty of good restaurants to choose from in the town

Tourist Information/ Oficina de Turismo

Tourist Office,
Place Général de Gaulle 14.
T: (0033) 0559 37 03 57

E:
saint.jean.pied.de.port@wanado
o.fr

W: www.terre-basque.com

Opening: Jul & Aug Mon–Sat
9am–12.30 & 2–7pm Sep–Jun
Mon–Sat 9am–noon & 2–7pm;

Post Office / Oficina de Correos

Main Post Office,
Rue de la Poste

Stage 1: St Jean Pied de Port - Roncesvalles
Map 1: Page 24 | Distance: 24km

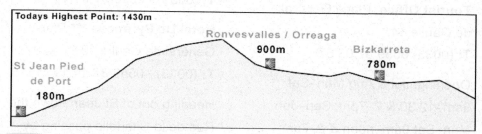

St Jean Pied de Port

798km to Santiago | Altitude: 180m | Population:1,400

St. Jean Pied de Port is a small picturesque walled town close to **Ostabat** in the French Pyrenean foothills, where three pilgrim routes, **Tours**, **Le Puy-en-Velay** and **Limoges**, converge.

The main street is the cobbled Rue de Citadelle which runs downhill past the **Eglise Notre Dame de St Jean Pied de Port** which has a fountain decorated with scallop shells outside and the **Porte Notre Dame**, the town gate.

Continuing on you will come to a bridge crossing the river Nive. From the bridge, there are beautiful views of the old houses with balconies overlooking the river.

At the top of the Rue de Citadelle you can visit what remains of the 17th Century Citadel, which has now been converted into a college.

Pilgrim Passport / Credencial

You can get your pilgrim passport / *credencial* from the pilgrim office Accueill at Rue de Citadelle 39

T: (0033) 0559 37 05 09.

It is open all day except at lunchtime.

Tourist Office, Place Général de Gaulle 14.
T: (0033) 0559 37 03 57

Opening: Jul & Aug Mon–Sat 9am–12.30 & 2–7pm; Sep–Jun Mon–Sat 9am–noon & 2–7pm;

Accommodation

Albergue Municipal, Rue de Citadelle 55 Beds: 18, Open all year round. Has a kitchen facility.

Albergue L'Esprit de Chemin, Rue de Citadelle 40.
T: (0033) - 0559 37 24 68
Beds: 18, Open Apr - Sept.
Offers dining services as well as lunch for the next days walk.

Albergue Esponda, Place du Trinquet 5.
T: (0033) - 0559 50 01 65
Beds: 20, Open all year round. Has a kitchen facility.

**Hotel Ramuntcho ** ** Rue de Citadelle 24.
T: (0033) - 0559 37 35 17

**Hotel Etche Ona ** ** Place Floquet 15.
T: (0033) - 0559 37 01 14

Hotel De Pyréneés * ** Place Général de Gaulle 19.
T: (0033) - 0559 37 11 19

Heading out of St Jean down the Rue de la Citadelle passing by the pilgrim office and through the archway, cross the bridge and onto Rue D'Espagne. At the **Porte d'Espagne**, an ancient gateway to Spain, you will see a signpost point out two possible routes.

The two routes are the Route de Napoleon, which makes it's way over the Pyrenees, and the Valcarlos route, which takes the lower roads making it a popular route for cyclists.

Valcarlos Route

The Valcarlos route is clearly marked and starts off along the River Nive along the D933. After 8km you'll come to **Arnéguy** on the France - Spain border. If you plan to stay here you can check the Arnéguy website for more details on accommodation. Most pilgrims will continue on for another 3km to Valcarlos.

Crossing the N135 onto the smaller road on the other side.

Continue on through **Óndarolle** down a steep hill across a bridge up to **Valcarlos/Luzaide.**

Valcarlos/Luzaide

Information

Valcarlos/Luzaide is made up of historical family villas and farms. The family homes are traditional with many whitewashed exteriors and family crests or coats of arms on the exterior.

Many of the locals have turned their homes into bed-and-breakfast style lodgings for the growing rural tourism industry in the Basque Country.

There is a modern monument to the pilgrimage road near the city hall representing a recumbent pilgrim. According to the locals Luzaide/Valcarlos is the true starting point for pilgrims in Spain who are traveling to Santiago.

Accommodation

Albergue, Calle Elizedea 52 Beds: 24, Open all year round. Has cooking facilities.

Leaving Valcarlos head up hill along the N135 until you cross the Río Chapital. Then turn left towards the small village of **Ganecoleta**. After walking a further 2 km along the side of the road take another left then climb up a steep hill through the beech

forests. After a further 2km you will return to the road turning left to reach **Puerta Ibañeta** where you will join the Route Napoléon.

Route de Napoléon

From the sign at Port d'Espagne

follow the sign for Chemin St Jacques passing a water fountain. The path climbs steeply along a country road. After 5km you will arrive at **Huntto**.

If you plan to stay here you can stay at the **Ferme Ithurburia** Quartier Huntto which has 18 beds
T: (0033) - 0559 37 11 17.

Leaving Huntto, turn left along a grass track, which climbs steeply until it joins the road. Turning left continue on till you pass a fountain on your right. The Camino levels out a bit and offers great panoramic views of the Pyrenees.

After a further 5km you come to **Auberge Orisson** which has 18 beds for €30 including dinner
T: (0033) - 0559 49 13 03.

Passing Auberge Orisson keep going uphill until you come to **Vierge d'Orisson** where you'll find statue of The Virgin / Vierge d'Orisson. Keep going along the road until you come to a

memorial cross on the right side of the road. The path now heads up a track onto a woodland path. Follow the signs to Fontaine de Roland after which you will pass a stone marker at the French - Spanish border.

You are now in the Navarra region of Spain. The camino takes you through scattered beech forest for a couple of kilometers until you reach **Col de Lepoeder**. From here you have another choice to make. There are two routes to Roncesvalles.

1. Puerta de Ibañeta Route

A longer route but a little kinder to the legs than the Roman Route, the Puerta de Ibañeta follows the sign at Col de Lepoeder to the right running along the road for 4km until you come to **Puerta de Ibañeta**.

From here head downhill for another 1.5km till you reach the Abbey in Roncesvalles.

2. Roman Route

A more direct path, the only problem being it does tend to get very steep.

Follow the path left from Col de Lepoeder, cross a small country road and keep a straight path downhill through the largest beech forest in Europe.

Some 3km later you will arrive at the Abbey in **Roncesvalles**.

 Roncesvalles

774km to Santiago | Altitude: 900m | Population:300

Information

Roncesvalles is a small village/hamlet with a population of around thirty. It has no shops apart from a bookshop, although it does have two hotels, a couple of bars, a tourist office, a monastery and

the church. Pilgrim Mass is held every evening at 8pm during the week and 6pm on weekends. You should try to book your evening meal at one of the bars before the evening service in the church.

The service in the church is conducted in a few languages and a blessing is given for all pilgrims setting out on their Camino to Santiago.

Tourist Office

In the old mill behind Casa Sabina

Accommodation

Albergue Municipal Beds: 120, Open all year round. Has a small kitchen.

Youth Hostel, In the monastery.

T: (0034) - 948 760 302/7

Beds: 78 in rooms of 6

Hostal La Posada **.

T: (0034) - 948 76 02 25

W:

www.posadaderoncesvalles.com

Hostal Casa Sabina **.

T: (0034) - 948 76 00 12

Stage 2: Roncesvalles - Larrasoaña

Map 1: Page 241 | Distance: 28km

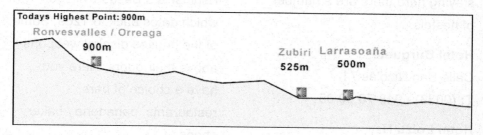

Roncesvalles

774km to Santiago | Altitude: 900m | Population: 300

Heading out of Roncesvalles take a left and walk for about 200m, you will see a map of the Camino at which point you take a right down a small woodland track. After walking for 2km this track takes you to the outskirts of **Burguete (Auritz)**

Burguete

771km to Santiago | Altitude: 900m | Population: 300

Information

Very attractive, 18th century houses dominate both sides of the main street of this pretty Basque village.

Ernest Hemingway lodged in Burguete during the 1920s and described it in his novel *The Sun Also Rises*. Hotel Burguette still has a piano with his signature on it.

The **Iglesia de San Nicolas de Barri** can be found in the centre of the village. Beside the church there's a nice cafe, Café Frontón, which serves breakfast.

Accommodation

Presently there are no albergues in Burguete but if you plan on staying here there are a number of hostels.

Hotel Burguete,
Calle San Nicolás 71.
T: (0033) - 948-76 00 05

Hotel Loizu Hs,
Avenida Roncesvales.
T: (0033) - 948-76 00 08

Hotel Juandeaburre, Calle San Nicolás 28. Tel: (0033) - 948-76 00 78

Leaving Burguete go down the main street past **Iglesia de San Nicolas de Bari** and the public garden. Take a right turn after 50m on the side of the Banco Central Hispano. Follow the track and cross the Río Urrobi.

Go straight to the footbridge over the stream, taking this track brings you to the road below **Iglesia San Bartolomé** and the tower of the *Bibliotheca Publica* on the other side of the road signposted to **Espinal**.

 # Espinal

Espinal is a Basque village, which dates back to 1269. Some of the houses display weapons above their doors. Here you have a choice of bars, restaurants, panaderia / bakery shops.

If you plan on staying here there is **Camping Urrobi, which** has bungalows for rent as well as a private albergue with 42 beds. Tel: (0033) 948-76 02 00

Turn right on the main road in the village. Pass the fountain and turn left at and take the small stretch of road uphill which takes you into the beech woods.

Fork right at the top, turn left through gate and continue right along gravel lane. Keep straight on this lane with a fence on the side of the field.

Leave the gate at end and cross the road at **Alto de Mezquiriz.**

After crossing the road do *not* go straight through the gate and up the track, instead take a left down a small footpath before you reach the fence.

Taking the left footpath takes you down through a gate to a lane, 60m later you reach a road at a bend. Take the old, shaded tunnel-like path and turn left at the fork then continue downhill through beech wood and across the Río Erro. Cross the road into the village of **Biskarreta**.

 # Biskarreta

Biskarreta is a small village with a shop and bar. You can get a pilgrim stamp, sello, at the church.

Casa Rural La Posada Nueva. **T:** (0033) 948 76 01 73

At the end of the village turn left at the shop and pass a small cemetery then take the middle of three small pathways, continue on until you cross a main road and take the path into Lintzoian.

Follow the road through village past the roofed *fronton* turn right uphill under a wooden footbridge over the road and keep straight on uphill on what becomes a stony lane.

Cross a road and keep going until you come to a Camino milestone marker, a yellow painted rock. Continue on to **Linzoáin** past the pelota court onto a woodland trail until you come to **Alto de Erro.**

Cross the main road. Keep straight on through more woods after 1km pass to the left of an old building; this is the *Venta del Caminante or Venta del Puerto,* a former pilgrim inn.

Continue downhill all the way to **Zubiri**.

 # Zubiri

752km to Santiago | Altitude: 525m | Population: 350

Information

In the Basque language, Zubiri means *village with the bridge.* The bridge itself is called *el Puente de la Rabia.*

Legend has it that any animal that crossed the bridge's central pillar three times would be cured from rabies.

The large building immediately to the right before the bridge was a former hospital, probably a leprosarium.

Accommodation

Albergue de Peregrinos de Zubiri (an old converted school), Avda. Zubir.
T: (0034) 626 501 582
Beds: 46. Has cooking facilities and Internet access.

Albergue Zaldiko, Puente de la Rabia.
T: (0034) 609 736 420
Beds: 24. Has washing facilities and Internet access.
W: www.alberguezaldiko.com

Leaving Zubiri on a well-marked path to a junction on gravel road near an industrial estate. As the factories come to an end take a right and walk down some steep steps.

Keep straight ahead and cross a stream and keep straight down the footpath. This leads uphill to the hamlet of **Ilarratz.**

Turn left at fountain and then right towards the hamlet of **Esquirotz.** On the other side of the hamlet follow a dirt track until it comes to a road. Cross it, go up a short flight of steps and keep straight onto a footpath through a field.

You'll come to a Camino map, here you can take a left to continue on the Camino or take a right to across Puente Larrasoaña into **Larrasoaña**

 Larrasoaña

746km to Santiago | Altitude: 500m | Population: 170

Information

Here you will see a statue of St James outside the **Iglesia de San Nicolás de Bari**.

Opposite the church is a large building which is the **Clavería de Roncesvalles**.

There are no shops or restaurants in Larrasoaña but the village bar is open for evening meals if you order in advance.

Accommodation

Albergue Municipal, Calle San Nicolás
Beds: 50. Run by the village mayor (*alcalde*) Don Santiago Zubiri Elizalde.

Hotel El Peregrino *, Calles San Nicolás 50.
T: (0034) 948 30 45 54

Hotel El Camino **, Calle San Nicholás 16.
T: (0034) 948 30 42 50

Stage 3: Larrasoaña - Pamplona

Map1 : Page 241 | Distance 13km

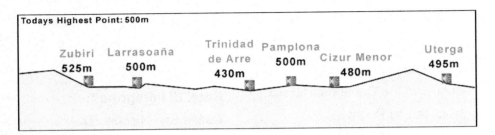

Todays Highest Point: 500m

Zubiri 525m Larrasoaña 500m Trinidad de Arre 430m Pamplona 500m Cizur Menor 480m Uterga 495m

 ## Larrasoaña

746km to Santiago | Altitude: 500m | Population: 170

Leave Larrasoaña across the Puente Larrasoaña, past the map of the camino. Take the track uphill and head straight on until you get to the vilage of **Aquerreta.**

There is the **Hotel Aquerreta ** T:** (0034) - 948 30 45 72, for those who might want to stay.

Follow the lane out of the village; cross a minor tarred road keep going straight. The track takes you through pinewoods parallel to the road.

You will come out onto farmland and you will then come to a modern bridge across the Río Agra and into the village of **Zuriáin.**

Continue along main road for about 400m and turn left and re-crossr the Río Arga. Take the right hand lane and continue on the path through more pine forest to the village of **Irotz.**

Heading out of Irotz cross the medieval bridge taking a left along the river. Continue on this path until you reach the village of **Zabaldika.**

Here you can see a statue of St James in the **Iglesia de San Esteban**.

Take the path that bypasses Zabaldica, cross the main road onto an old road. Turn right at a resting/picnic area and take the track uphill, parallel to the river until you arrive at the small village of **Arleta**.

Follow the way marks for 1km until you get to the main road and pass via a tunnel underneath the road. Turn right onto the service road and after a few hundred yards you reach a medaeival bridge over the Río Ulzama at **Trinidad de Arre**

 # Trinidad de Arre

737.5km to Santiago | Altitude: 430m | Population: 9800

Information

On the other side of the bridge you will find the **Basilica de la Trinidad de Arre**, which has a monastery and an albergue.

Accommodation

Albergue Municipal, Basilica de Arre. **Beds:** 30. Open all year round. Has kitchen & washing facilities.

Turn left at the end of the bridge and walk along the Calle Mayot which leads into **Villava.**

Villava

Villava is a suburb of Pamplona but there is still a bit to go before reaching the center of the city.

Go along the main street past the public gardens and cross the road at the traffic lights. Continue straight on until you reach the suburb of **Burlada**.

You come to a set of traffic lights, cross the road and turn right along the Calle Larraizar. You'll see a school on your right, just before you reach the main road. Cross the road and keep walking straight on the Carretera Burlada. You'll pass two houses decorated with scallop shells,

Casa de las Conchas. As you get close to the Río Agra turn right and then take a left over the mediaeval Puente de Magdelena.

On the other side of the bridge pass a fountain and then cross the public gardens, Playa Caparroso, towards the city walls.

Walk over the drawbridge and through the impressive city gates, Portal de Zumalacárregi and into the old town of **Pamplona**.

 # Pamplona

733km to Santiago | Altitude: 500m | Population: 196,000

Information

Inside the city walls you can take a left into Plaza San José to the **Catedral of Santa María la Real**, the albergue opens at 01:00pm. Or you can continue straight into Calle Carmen until you come to a junction.

Turn right along Calle Mercederes to the city center or turn left onto Calle Curia towards the cathedral and a pilgrim hostel.

Pamplona (Iruña) is the capital city of Navarra. It has a population of around 171,150, and is 92 kilometres from the town of San Sebastián, and 407 kilometres from Madrid. Behind it's impressive city walls you'll find Pamplona's most important building, the fourteenth century gothic cathedral, which is definitely worth a visit. There are another two main Gothic churches in the old city, San Sernin and San Nicolás, which were both, built during the thirteenth century.

On the 6th July at midnight the famous **Fiesta de San Fermín** starts. During this festival *el encierro/running of the bulls,* made famous by Ernest Hemingway, takes place. He was honoured for this by having a street in the city named after him, Paseo Hemingway.

El Encierro involves hundreds of people running in front of six bulls and another six steers down an 825-metre (0.51 mile) stretch of narrow streets of a section of the old town of Pamplona towards the bull ring.

Accommodation in the city is very hard to find during the festival and expect prices to treble in most places. Albergues will not be open during this period so it is probably best to not to be walking through Pamplona during the festival.

History

The Romans called the city Pompaelo, after it's founder Pompey. By 409 Pamplona was controlled by the Visigoths and then for a brief period by the Muslims.

By the 8th century it had become the center of the kingdom of Navarra and by the end of the 10th century it's position on the Camino de Santiago assured it's prosperity. During the Spanish Civil war, Pamplona along with the rest of Navarra sided with Franco and the Nationalists.

Layout

Pamplona has maintained the medieval layout of the town, including a star fort. The old city is very compact and is bordered to the north and east by the Río Arga and by the remains of the old walls, and to the west by parks and the old citadel.

The city is home to two universities, the Universidad de Navarra, founded by Opus Dei in 1952, and the Universidad Pública de Navarra, created by the government of Navarra in 1987.

Most of the cheapest accommodation is in the streets

west of the main square, Plaza Del Castillo. Everything incuding the bus station and the bullring is a short walk from here. The train station however is on the other side of the river, north west of the center.

Accommodation

Remember: During San Fermin Festival 6th July - 14th July, accommodation prices treble and is extremely hard to find. Albergues are closed during the festival.

Albergue Jesús y Maria,
Calle Compañia 4
Beds: 110. Open Apr - Oct. Has cooking & laundry facilities.

Albergue Paderborn,
Playa de Caparroso.
T: (0034) 948 22 15 58
Beds: 28. Open Apr - Oct. Has dining facilities.

Pension Acella II,
Calle Acella, 11 6° B.
T: (0034) - 948 26 10 00 / 948 17 33 48
E: acella@ono.com

Pension Acella III,
Calle Acella, 11 6° B.
T: (0034) - 948 26 10 00 / 948 17 33 48
E: acella@ono.com

Pension Acella IV,
Calle Pintor Paret, 2 2° E.
T: (0034) - 948 26 10 00 / 948 17 33 48 / 619 78 69 99
E: acella@ono.com
W: www.hostalacella.com

Hotel Eslava,
Plaza de la Virgen de la O 7.
T: (0034) 948 22 22 70
E: correo@hotel-eslava.com
W: www.hotel-eslava.com

Hotel Pamplona Plaza,
Avenida Marcelo Celayeta, 35.
T: (0034) 948 13 60 12
E: reservas@hotelpamplonaplaza.com
W: www.hotelpamplonaplaza.com

Hotel Yoldi, Avenida San Ignacio / San Inazio Etorbidea 11.

T: (0034) 948 22 48 00

E: yoldi@hotelyoldi.com

W:www.hotelyoldi.com

Check: http://tinyurl.com/hotels-pamplona

Where to Eat

The cuisine of Pamplona has an excellent reputation and is extremely varied thanks to the characteristics of its surrounding landscapes.

Specialties are several preparations of game, usually in tasty sauces, as well as salmon and trout. An original recipe is trout filled with cured ham.

Also **Pochas de Sangúesa**, a very delicious kind of beans of high reputation, is the base of many typical dishes.

The region is famous for its dishes of lamb and goat: Asados de Cordero, Cabrito and Cordero en Chilindrón.

It also has delicious vegetables, like the mild Pimientos del Piquillo (red pepper) and Asparagus, as well as an original preparation of fish in a sauce of garlic and paprika, called **Ajoarriero**.

The dishes mentioned above should be combined with one of the well-known wines of the region of Navarra.

Pamplona has an enormous variety of options for eating out, from sandwiches in bars to a meal in a fancy restaurant. Remember that prices rise quite considerably during the fiesta.

Local meal times are generally 2:00pm - 3:00pm for lunch and 9:00pm - 10.30 pm for dinner.

Tourist Information/ Oficina de Turismo

The Tourist Office, Calle del Duque de Ahumada 3.

Opening: Mon - Fri 10:00am - 14:00pm then 16:00pm - 19:00pm Sat 10:00am - 14:00

Post Office / Oficina de Correos

Main Post Office, Paseo de Sarasate

Opening hours: **Mon – Fri:** 08:00 - 20:30 **Sat:** 09:30 - 14:00

No service on July 6th, 7th and Sundays.

Medical & Emergency Services

Emergency Number for all services: 112

Hospital de Navarra:

Calle Irunlarrea, 3

T: (0034) 848 422 100

Hospital Virgen del Camino:

Calle Irunlarrea, 4

T: (0034) 848 429 400

Stage 4: Pamplona - Puente la Reina

Map 1 : Page 241 Distance 23.5km

Todays Highest Point: 735m

Pamplona 500m | Cizur Menor 480m | Uterga 495m | Obanos 410m | Puente la Reina 350m | Cirauqui 486m | Lorca 462m | Estella 425m

 Pamplona

🅰 🄷 🍴 ☕ € 🛒 ℹ ➕

733km to Santiago | Altitude: 500m | Population: 196,000

The Camino is well marked through Pamplona. Turning off the Calle del Carmen at a small plaza keep straight on along the Calle del Carmen, turning right into the Calle de Mercadores

Continue to the Plaza Consistorial then turn right into the Calle san Saturnino and keep straight until you come out at parkland surrounding the Cuidadela. Follow the flagstone path and when it turns in front of

Pamplona's *Cuidadel* (citadel) take a right onto the road and follow the markers on towards Cizur Meno.

You'll come to a bridge over the Río Sadar, cross over and then again over the Río Elorz. Keep straight on crossing a railway track, go to the top of the hill, which descends into the village of **Cizur Menor**.

Cizur Menor

728.5km to Santiago |
Altitude: 480m | Population:
700

Information

The 13th Century **Iglesia San Miguel Archángel** has been restored; it was once converted into a warehouse.

The doorway is Romanesque - Gothic in style with a Greek monogram of Christ in the tympanum. The Romanesque parish church is on the right and has also been recently restored.

There are several bars and restaurants in the area as well as a chemist, *farmacia*.

Accommodation

Albergue De Maribel, just up from the crossroads.
T: (0034) 948 18 83 85
Beds: 50. Open all year. Has cooking & washing facilities as well as a nice garden to relax in. Run by the kind and hospitable Roncal family on the grounds of their home.

Albergue Orden de Malta.
T: (0034) 600 38 68 91
Beds: 27 in 3 rooms. Open from Jun - Sep. Has kitchen facilities.

Leaving Cizur Menor take the main road downhill and then right down footpath on the left hand side of the *frontón* and turn left.

Keep on straight heading towards the line of 40ish wind turbines on the Alto de Pérdon. These turbines provide Pamplona with some of it's electricity supply.

The Camino now takes you to the church and through the village of **Guendulâin**, across a stream bypassing the ruins of Guendulâin Palace. Keep on towards the turbines across a minor road. Go straight uphill towards the top of Alto de

Pérdon and the village of **Zariquiegui.** On the way up you get a great view of Pamplona.

Zariquiegui's 13th century Romanesque **Iglesia de San Andrés** is on your right as you walk into the village. You will also pass a splendid fountain. As you leave the village the paths takes you left and uphill to the **Alto de Perdón** and the line of wind turbines. Just before you get to the top you pass the **Fuente Reniega (**Fountain of Renouncement).

Legend has it that a tired and thirsty pilgrim was confronted by the devil disguised as a fellow pilgrim The devil offered to show him a hidden fountain on the condition that he renounced God, the Virgin Mary and St James. The pilgrim refused and St James, disguised as a pilgrim, came to his rescue and led him to a hidden fountain where he was able to quench his thirst with the help of his scallop shell.

Passing the fountain you arrive at Alto de Perdón. On your right you will see an iron sculpture depicting a parade of male and female pilgrims, horses, donkeys and dogs all making their way to Santiago.

From here you can see the next village of Uterga as well as Obanos and on a clear day Puente la Reina.

Crossing to the other side of the road follow the way marks down a stony track, which leads to the base of the valley through vineyards and almond trees.

Keep going straight on, cross a small river and walk uphill into the village of **Uterga.**

Uterga

716.5km to Santiago |
Altitude: 495m

Accommodation

Albergue Municipal,
Plaza Mayor.
Beds: 4. Open all year round

Albergue Camino del Perdón.
T: (0034) 948 34 46 61
Beds: 16. Open all year round
and serves food.

Go straight through the Uterga,
passing the Albergue Camino del
Perdón and continue along a
quiet road for 2km to the village
Muruzabal.

Muruzábal

714.5km to Santiago |
Altitude: 420m

You pass an almond grove on
your right as you enter the
village. Walk past a *frontón* and
the walled **Iglesia de San
Estaban**.

In the main square you will find a
bar and a chemist / *farmacia*.
Pass through the village and
take a right at a metal cross and
walk along the side of some
fields.

Continue on to the top of a hill
and take a right, which will lead
you into **Obanos** passing the
Iglesia de San Juan Bautista
and the albergue.

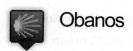

Obanos

712.5km to Santiago |
Altitude: 410m | Population:
800

Information

It is well worth taking a walk
through the beautiful streets and
squares of Obanos. You'll find a
grocery shop and a butcher shop
near the church.

Its monuments include the
**Nuestra Señora de Arnotegui
Shrine**, where the legend of the
Mystery of San Guillén and
Santa Felicia has its origins.

This story is closely linked to the
Camino de Santiago and is
played out by 800 locals every
two years in July.

**Legend of the Mystery of
San Guillén and Santa
Felicia**

"Of Santa Felicia's martyrdom
and San Guillén's penance",

gives name to a legend of the
14th century. It's the story of the
Duke of Aquitanie's children.

After going on pilgrimage on the
way to St. James, the princess
Felicia felt religious vocation and
decided to abandon the comforts
of the court and live the life of a
hermit in Navarra. Her brother
Guillén found her and killed her,
after her refusal to assume her
class responsibilities. Santa
Felicia's grave is in Labiano
(Aranguren Valley).

Guillén obtained sanctity after
going on a pilgrimage to
Santiago de Compostela and
spent the rest of his life in the
close to Obanos Arnotegui
Hermitage, consoling the
pilgrims of the Camino de
Santiago and helping the poor,

where his relics are still worshipped.

Accommodation

Albergue, Calle San Larenzo 6 **Beds:** 36. Open from Apr - Oct. Has cooking facilities.

Hostel Osses * San Guillermo 3. **T:** (0034) 948 34 42 61

Leaving Obanos proceed straight to Calle San Juan then turn right into Calle Julian Gayarre.

Take a left and continue through an archway and go straight, following the road as it bends to the right passing the town *frontón* and fountain opposite.

At the **Ermita San Salvador** the road becomes a rough track running along the side of a farm. Keep straight on until you come to the main road. Cross over and turn left down a footpath through some allotments. You will then rejoin the road by Hotel Jacque, which is an albergue as well as an hotel. There is a modern statue of Santiago Peregrino at the junction of the Camino Frances and the Camino Aragonés. Turn left after about 300m along the Carretera Pamplona for 300m to **Puente la Reina (Gares)**.

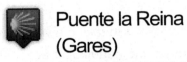 # Puente la Reina (Gares)

709.5km to Santiago | Altitude: 350m | Population: 2,500

Information

Puente la Reina's main albergue is the first building on your left opposite the Romanesque **Iglesia del Crucifijo**.

Puente La Reina (*Ponte de Arga*) got its name at the beginning of the eleventh century. Doña Mayor, wife of Sancho "el Fuerte" III (though it may also have been Doña Estefania wife of Don Garcia,

Doña Mayor's niece) was the queen who gave her name to the town. She built the six-arched bridge over the Río Arga for the use of pilgrims going to Santiago de Compostela.

Puente la Reina doesn't have the plazas and squares you find in most other towns in Navarra. The main monuments can be found along the Calle Mayor.

The **Iglesia del Crucifijo**, built in the twelfth century by the Knights Templar, had a second nave added three centuries later to house an impressive Y-shaped gothic crucifix carried from Germany by a pilgrim.

Two towers flank one end of the Calle Major. On both sides all the way there are palaces, large houses decorated with shields, projecting eaves and graceful balconies covered with geraniums.

At the other end, a fortified gateway gives access to the famous six-arched Romanesque

bridge, a superb example of mediaeval construction. The bridge gave its name to the town.

You should make a point of checking out the facade of the **Iglesia de Santiago**. It has Moorish influence in its south portal, carved with saints & sinners, and gargoyles.

Inside the church you can see a Baroque painting depicting scenes from the life of Saint James. In the left hand aisle you'll find a statue of Santiago Peregrino, also known in Basque as Santiago Beltza (Black Santa)

Tourist Office,
Calle Mayor, 105.
T: (0034) 948 34 08 45
E: turismo@puentelareina-gares.es
W: www.puentelareina-gares.es

Accommodation

Albergue Seminario,
Calle Crucifijo 1
Beds: 100. Open all year round.
Has cooking facilities.

Albergue Santiago Apostol,
cross the bridge at the far end of
the town.
T: (0034) 948 34 02 20
Beds: 100. Open from Easter -
Oct. Has dining facilities.

Camping El Real,
Paraje El Real.
T: (0034) 948 34 02 20
Has bungalows for 5 - 8 people
available from April - October.
E: campingelreal@hotmail.com
W: www.campingelreal.com

Albergue Jakue,
Calle Irunbidea.
T: (0034) - 948 34 10 17
Beds: 40. Open all year round.
Has cooking facilities.
Albergue Jakue also has hostel
rooms available and a

restaurant.
E: hotel@jakue.com
W: www.jakue.com

Hotel Bidean ** Calle Mayor, 20.
T: (0034) 948 34 04 57 / 948 34
11 56
E: info@bidean.com
W: www.bidean.com

Stage 5: Puente la Reina - Estella

Map 2: Page 242 | Distance: 25.5km

 ## Puente la Reina

709.5km to Santiago |
Altitude: 350m | Population:
2,500

Leave Puente la Reina crossing
the bridge, turn left and cross the
main road.

You'll pass a convent,
**Comendadores del Espíritu
Santo** and the **Barrio de las
Monjas** then onto a track that
runs along the Río Arga.

You'll pass a factory after a few
kilometers. Follow the track uphill
then go through some fields, you
then pass the site of 13th century

Monasterio de Bargota where
you'll find a fountain and a
modern picnic area. Continue on,
passing a roundabout, and follow
the yellow arrow way markers
over a bridge into **Mañeru**.

 ## Mañeru

703km to Santiago | Altitude:
455m

Information

As you enter the village you will
see a medieval *cruceiro* (cross).
To your right you will see the
Iglesia de San Pedro which
houses an 18th century Baroque
painting.

Near the church you'll find two bars and two shops.

Accommodation

Refugio de los Padres Reparadores, beside the Monastery. **Beds:** 33.

Casa Rural Isabel, Caridad 10. **T:** (0034) - 948 34 02 83

Hostal Jakue
Beds: 20. Serves supper from 07:00pm

Heading out of the village along the Calle de la Esperanza into the Plaza de los Fueros and turn left at the end of Casa Consistoria then a right and continue on Calle Forzosa straight through olive groves and vineyards.

After you pass a cemetery, keep straight on. The path takes you through an arch into to the hilltop village of **Cirauqui**.

Cirauquí

700km to Santiago | Altitude: 486m

Information

Cirauqui is a mediaeval village whose cobbled streets take you up to the old part of the village and to the 12th century **Iglesia de San Román**, which has an impressive Romanesque doorway.

You will also find the **Iglesia de Santa Catalina** and a Roman bridge nearby.

If you are passing through Cirauqui between the 13th & 19th of September you will see the locals celebrating **Día de la Cruz (Day of the Cross)**

Accommodation

Albergue Maralotz, Calle
Román 30.
T: (0034) - 678 63 52 08
Beds: 28. Opens Mar to Oct.

You can book rooms in advance.
Serves dinner and breakfast.

Leaving Cirauqui through an
arch, the Camino route runs
along a tree lined track downhill
onto an old paved Roman road,
which crosses the river on the
Roman bridge. Continue on until
you reach the main road. Cross
the road onto a dirt track and
follow this path through farmland
and over hills, passing the site of
a mediaeval bridge and the
medieval route of a well-
preserved Roman road.

On reaching the brow of the hill,
keep straight on along the edges
of farm fields. Take the right
hand path along the Roman road
continuing to the junction of a
minor road to your right, passing
underneath it twice.

Follow this road under a high
modern aquaduct, and then turn
left onto a path, which leads you
over the Río Salado via an old
restored mediaeval bridge.

Take the path from the bridge
under the road again then go
straight up into the village of
Lorca.

 # Lorca

693.5km to Santiago |
Altitude: 462m
Lorca has a population of around
140, it has a nice plaza with a
fountain and if you wish to stay
there are two albergues.

Accommodation

Albergue José Ramón,
Calle Mayor, 40.
T: (0034) - 948 51 11 90
Beds: 14. Open from Easter -
Oct.
Has dining & washing facilities
as well as internet access.

La Bodega del Camino,
Calle Mayor.
T: (0034) - 948 54 11 62

Beds: 36. Open all year round.
Offers cooking & dining facilities,
washing and Internet. Also
operates as a hotel.
E: info@labodegadelcamino.com
W:www.labodegadelcamino.com

Go through village past the
church and down the main street
along a narrow track through
cornfields and next to the road.

Follow this track passing through
a tunnel and then across an
arched Romanesque bridge over
the Río Nueva into the village of
Villatuerta.

Villatuerta

688km to Santiago | Altitude:
486m

Head uphill to the 12th century
Iglesia de la Asuncíon, which is
an ideal place for a rest. If
needed there is a fountain with
safe drinking water (aqua
potable) to the left of the church
gate. There is also a statue of
San Veremundo to the right.

The route leaving Villatuerta
follows a path uphill past farm
buildings and through fields and
passes close to the **Ermita de**

San Miguel. You'll come to a
picnic area, cross the main road
here and take the path until you
come to a small footbridge
across a stream. When you
reach a factory building turn right
and continue until you pass the
Iglesia del Santo Sepulcro with
its impressive 14th century

Gothic doorway. Continue straight on into **Estella** and after the Puente de los Peregrinos you'll see the Albergue Municipal.

 Estella / Lizarra

684km to Santiago | Altitude: 425m | Population: 13,000

Information

The picturesque town of Estella / Lizarra is situated on the bed of the Río Arga. The village of Lizarra acquired its Castilian name, Estella, in 1090 when Sancho Ramírez, King of Aragón & Navarra, made it the main reception point for pilgrims walking the Camino de Santiago.

The towns **Tourist Office**, Calle de San Nicolás 1, **T:** (0034) - 948 55 40 11 open Mon - Fri during the months of Apr - Sep. They organise regular guided tours of the town and are situated amongst some of the towns most important buildings.

The tower of the 13th Century **Iglesia de**

San Pedro de la Rúa is the most prominent building in Estella. You can visit the partly ruined cloister but first you need to ask at the tourist office.

Beside the tourist office is a rare example of 12th century Romanesque construction, the **Palacio de los Reyes de Navarra**.

It is now home to the **Museo de Gustavo de Maetzu**, a small free gallery open from Tue - Sat 11:00am - 01:00pm then from 05:00pm - 07:00pm

Across the Río Arga and overlooking Estella is the **Iglesia de San Miguel**, which features an elaborate Romanesque door depicting the Last Judgment.

Most of Estella's bars and shops are on this side of the river.

Accommodation

Albergue de Peregrinos.
Calle La Rúa, 50.
T: (0034) - 948 55 02 00
Beds: 10. Open all year round.
Has cooking & washing facilities as well as Internet access.
E: luisnavarroplo@hotmail.com

Albergue Municipal Oncineda,
Calle Monasterio de Irach.
T: (0034) - 948 55 50 22
Beds: 15. Open all year round.
Has dining, cooking & washing facilities as well as internet access.
E:albergueoncineda@escur.com
W: www.escur.com

Fonda Izarra,
Calle Caldereria 20.
T: (0034) - 948 55 06 78

Fonda San Andrés,
Plaza Santiago 1.
T: (0034) - 948 55 41 58

Hostal Cristina,
Calle Baja Navarra 1.
T: (0034) - 948 55 07 72

Hostal El Volante,
Calle Merkatondoa,2 1ª Planta.
T: (0034) - 948 55 39 57 / 638 029 005)
E: hostalelvolante@gmail.com
W: www.hostalelvolante.com

Stage 6: Estella - Los Arcos

Map 2: Page 242 | Distance: 20.5km

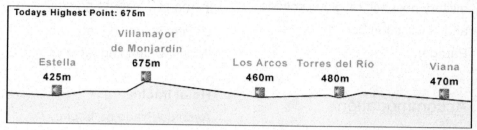

Todays Highest Point: 675m

Villamayor
de Monjardín

Estella	675m	Los Arcos	Torres del Río	Viana
425m		460m	480m	470m

 Estella

684km to Santiago | Altitude: 425m | Population: 13,000

Heading out of Estella pass the Albergue Municipal Oncineda through the Puerta de Castilla across the road and head uphill to **Ayegui**

 Ayegui

682km to Santiago | Altitude: 485m

Information

Head towards the **Monasterio de Irache**. You'll come to the **Fuente del Vino**, free red wine on tap provided by Bodegas Irache. A perfect start to a days walking!

You can watch the thirsty pilgrims here **www.irache.com/webcam.html**

Beside the tap is the Monasterio de Irache, one of the most important monumental complexes in Navarra.

Over the years it has been a pilgrims' hospice, university, military hospital, religious college and, it will soon become a Parador.

Accommodation

Albergue Municipal,
Calle Polideportiv.
T: (0034) - 948 55 43 11
Beds: 90. Open all year round. Has dining & washing facilities as well as Internet access.

Follow the track out of Ayegui past vineyards into **Irache.**

Irache

681km to Santiago |
Altitude: 573

Information

Irache is a small town of modern houses with a large camping complex, which also offers rooms, and a hotel.

Accommodation

Camping Iratx,
T: (0034) - 948 55 55 55
E: info@campingiratxe.com
W: www.campingiratxe.com

Hotel Irache,
Avenida Prado de Irache, 7.
T: (0034) - 948 55 11 50
E: info@hotelirache.com
W: www.hotelirache.com

Heading through Irache you walk along some fields and through a kermes oak wood woods. The path crosses a local road and, once out of the wood, follows a track until it reaches **Azqueta.**

Continue on through village, and head downwards and pass in front of a dairy.

The track leads to the Gothic fountain, Fuente de los Moros, of **Villamayor de Monjardín**.

Continue on until you reach the village situated at the foot of its famous ruined castle.

Villamayor de Monjardín

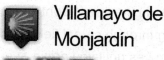

675.5km to Santiago | Altitude: 675m | Population: 150

Information

At an altitude of 650m Villamayor de Monjardín has great view over the surrounding countryside. The ruins of **Castillo de San Esteban** over look the vilage from the top of Monjardín.

The Town Hall, a former school and jail (at different times of course), was restored in 1987. It consists of two floors: On the first there is the meeting lounge, the archives, an office, and the bathrooms. On the second there is a store. On the ground floor there is a bar.

You will also find the **Fuente de los Moros** (Fountain of the Moors), a precious Romanesque cistern of the 12th century with a rectangular floor and stairs descending to the spring. An impressive vault starts from the interior forming two pointed arches. The Institution of the Prince of Viana in 1991 restored it.

The **Iglesia de San Andrés** is a Romanesque building with some of the pre-gothic structure dating to the 12th century. It consists of a single nave composed of various sections ending in an ample front where there is a window.

A very important element of this church is the Romanesque doorway with its archivolts, monogram of Christ, and scenes depicting the battle between the two knights (Charlemagne and a Navarran Prince).

Accommodation

Albergue Parroquial Santa Cruz, At Village Entrance
Beds: 26. Open Apr - Oct. Has

cooking facilities and price includes dinner and breakfast.

Albergue Hogar de Monjardín,
In front of the church in the square.
T: (0034) - 948 53 71 36
Beds: 20

Leave Villamayor de Monjardín passing by the church and heading along a concrete path that soon heads downhill until it reaches a wider track. Cross the local road and continue on a gravel path along flat land, between vineyards, cereal fields, and small pinewoods.

The track continues past the ancient Fuente del Pozode Baurín around a hill on which the Corral Santo (Holy Enclosure) is found.

A little further on the route makes a right turn and crosses the fields until it reaches the other side of a watercourse, approaching a small hill range covered with replanted pine trees. Continue walking through cereal fields and olive groves until you arrive at a fountain on the outskirts of the town.

Take the left hand fork in the road and walk along the Calle Mayor into **Los Arcos**

 Los Arcos

663.5km to Santiago | Altitude: 460m | Population: 1,300

Information

Los Arcos is located on the foot of a hill on the banks of the Río Odrón. Taking a short walk around the town you can discover all that this beautiful village has to offer.

In addition to it's most beautiful building the **Iglesia de Santa María**, you will see the Estanco and the Santa María doorways.

The last is dating from the 17th century. After mass pilgrims can climb to the church's Renaissance bell tower.

If you cross the Los Arcos streets and squares you will find several baroque mansions and manor houses dating from the 17th & 18th century.

Los Arcos has three hermitages, the Calvario - an 18th century baroque building, the San Sebastián and the San Blas.

Tourist Information,
Calle Fueros
T: (0034) 948 42 77 53

Accommodation

Albergue Casa Alberdi,
Calle El Hortal 3.
T: (0034) 948 64 07 64 / 650 96 52 50
Beds: 22. Open all year round. Cooking & washing facilities as well as Internet access.

Albergue Isaac Jacob,
Calle San Lázaro.
T: (0034) 948 44 10 91
Beds: 72. Open from Easter - Oct. Has Kitchen facilities.

Albergue la Fuente - Casa de Austria, Calle Travesía del Estanco 5.
T: (0034) 948 64 07 97
Beds: 40.Open all year round. Has kitchen, dining & washing facilities and also has Internet access.

Albergue Romero,
Calle Mayor 19.
T: (0034) - 948 64 00 83
Beds: 28. Open all Year round. Has kitchen & washing facilities as well as breakfast services

Hostal Ezequiel **,

Calle La Serna 14.

T: (0034) - 948 64 02 96

E: reservas@hostalezequiel.com

W: www.hostalezequiel.com

Hostal Suetxe **,

Calle Carramendavia.

T: (0034) - 948 44 11 75

E: recepcion@suetxe.com

W: www.suetxe.com

Hotel Mónaco **,

Plaza del Coso 1.

T: (0034) - 948 64 00 00

E: info@hotelmonaco.es

W: www.hotelmonaco.es

Pension Mavi - Mavi Boarding House, Calle del Medio 7.

T: (0034) - 948 640 081 / 608 934 222

E: info@pensionmavi.es

W: www.pensionmavi.es

Stage 7: Los Arcos - Logroño
Map 2: Page 242 | Distance: 30km

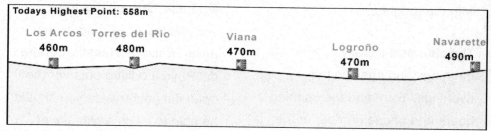

Los Arcos

663.5km to Santiago | Altitude: 460m | Population: 1,300

Information

Leave Los Arcos past the cemetery and church through an arch and cross the Río Odrón. Continue through farmland and vineyards to the little hamlet of **Sansol.**

Sansol
Information

Sansol has some fine examples of Baroque architecture from the large houses to the Iglesia de San Zoilo. Leaving Sansol cross over the main road and downhill to a stone brdge across the Río Linares then uphill into the village of **Torre del Río**.

Torre del Río

644km to Santiago | Altitude: 480m | Population: 180

Information

Torres del Rio is situated in the Río Linares valley. It's best known for its pretty octagonal 12th century Iglesia de Santo Sepulcro, which is thought to be linked to the Knights Templar.

The design of the church is similar to the style associated with the Knights.

The church is usually open in the mornings and again in the evenings. You'll find the opening hours and phone number of the church guardian posted on the door. The guardian may open the church for you if you ask nicely enough and offer a small donation / donativo.

Accommodation

Albergue Casa Mari,
Cale Casa Nueva 13.
T: (0034) 948 64 80 18
Beds: 21 in 4 rooms. Open all year round. Has cooking & laundry facilities as well as Internet access.

Head out of Torre del Río passing a cemetery out onto a dirt track. Stay on this track until you join the main road as you pass Ermita de Nuestra Señora del Poyo. Looking out over the open flat countryside you should be able to catch a glimpse of Viana and Logroño.

Cross the main road once again and climb up a dirt track that leads us to the road to Bargota. On the other side of this road, drop down into the little Cornava valley, whose watercourse you follow downwards and cross further on.

From here head up again and over the main road straight to Viana. Cross back over the road and through the outskirts of Viana and climb up into the centre of **Viana** on Calle Algorrada passing through an archway in the town walls and then onto the Rua de Santa María.

Viana

A H ⑪ 🍴 € ⓘ 🛒 ➕ @

633.5km to Santiago |
Altitude: 470m | Population:
3500

Information

King Sancho III 'El Fuerte'
officially founded Viana in 1219
with a clearly defensive
objective. Situated on a hill, the
layout is that of a fortified square,

with narrow streets surrounded
by part of its thick medieval wall.
Today Viana is a lively own with
a population of around 3,500.

The majestic Iglesia de Santa
María is one of the most
impressive buildings in the town.
It was built between 1250 and
1312 in Gothic style with the
tower and the southern doorway
added, in Renaissance style, in
the 16th century. At the foot of
the church, under the slabs of

the atrium, lie the remains of the
soldier, prince and cardinal
Cesare Borgia, who died close to
Viana in 1507. The church is on
the Plaza de los Fueros, which
has a nice fountain at its centre
and plenty of cafes.

Although the 13th-century Iglesia
de San Pedro is in ruins its
Baroque façade dating from the
18th century is still in good
condition. From here you get a
good view of the medieval walls
and the nearby lands of La Rioja
and Álava.

Tourist Information,
Plaza de los Fueros 1.
T: (0034) 948 44 63 02

Accommodation

**Albergue Municipal Andrés
Muñoz**, Calle San Pedro.
T: (0034) 948 64 50 37 / 948 64
55 30
Beds: 54. Open all year round.
Has cooking & laundry facilities
as well as Internet access.

Albergue Santa Maria,
Plaza de los Fueros.
Beds: 16. Open Jun - Oct. Has
cooking & dining facilities.

Hostal Casa Armendáriz **,
Calle Navarro Villoslada 19.
T: (0034) 948 64 50 78

Hostal San Pedro **,
Calle Medio San Pedro 13.
T: (0034) 948 44 62 21

Hotel Palacio de Pujadas ***,
Calle Navarro Villoslada 30.
T: (0034) 948 64 64 64

Leave Viana through the
mediaeval stone arch of Portal
San Felices and turn left down
Calle la Rueda and through the
suburbs until you get back to the
main road. Cross over onto a
quiet dirt track, which passes
through fields until you reach the
Ermitas de las Cuevas.

Beside the old hermitage there's
a picnic area with a fountain. At
the end of the picnic area follow

the track to Laguna de las Cañas
taking you to the main road.
Cross over to a path, which runs
parallel to the road through fields
and past a factory into the region
of La Rioja.

Head under the ring road
towards Cerro de Cantabria.
Follow the new paved track
gently up the flat-topped hill,
which is home to the mediaeval
ruins of the prehistoric city of

Cantabria. Excavations are still
ongoing on the site. Head
downhill passing the Casa de
Chozo where a lady called Felisa
will stamp your passport /
credencial whilst you enjoy some
welcome refreshments.

Continue of for 1km then turn left
across a stone bridge Puente de
Piedra over the Río Ebro. The
bridge was restored in 1880,
replacing the mediaeval pilgrim
bridge that dates back to the
11th century and was later
repaired by Santa Domingo and

San Juan de Ortega. At the other side of the bridge turn right and down Calle Rua Vieja past the Iglesia Maria del Palacio into **Logroño**.

 # Logroño

A H A 🍴 🍵 € i 🛒 ✚ @

633.5km to Santiago | Altitude: 470m | Population: 148,000

Information

Logroño, the capital of La Rioja, is a busy university city with a population of around 150,000. It is also at the centre of the regions wine industry.

As well as it's wine industry; Logroño also makes a living from the production of metal and textiles. The **Iglesia de Santiago el Real** is located on the Camino route at the end of Calle Rúa Vieja.

Above the entrance Santiago Matamoros (Santiago, the Moor slayer) depicted riding into battle. The building is on the site of a 9th century church built to honour the battle of Clavijo where Santiago Matamoros helped defeat the Moors.

Inside, the image of the Virgen de la Esperanza, Logroño's patron saint, is displayed. Along the same street you'll find the famous pilgrim's fountain along with many carvings related to the Camino.

The **Catedral de Santa María de la Redonda** is built on the site of an old circular Romanesque church in the Plaza del Mercado. Its two Baroque towers rise high above the market square and are currently home to a couple of large storks nests.

Inside the cathedral are the carvings of Gregorio Fernández and a representation of the way of the cross by the Renaissance maestro Michelangelo. The cathedral is open from 08:15am - 13:15pm and 18:30- 19:00.

You'll also find a few cafes scattered around the square.

The **Iglesia de Santa María de Palacio**, found next to the hostel, is the oldest church in Logroño. It's Gothic pyramid tower, **Aguja** as it is locally known, dominates the capital's skyline and has become the emblem of the city. Inside the church are magnificent cloisters and several Romanesque pieces to admire.

The 12th century **Iglesia San Bartolomé** with its distinctive Mudejar tower is nearby. Devoted to the patron saint of the city, it preserves an exquisite Romanesque sculptured front, the only example of Romanesque art in the city.

Logroño also has fine examples of civil architecture, such as the **Palacio de la Marquis of**

Legarda, **Los Chapiteles** or the **Museo de La Rioja**, which can be found in the 18th century Baroque **Palacio de Espartero**.

The **Paséo del Espolón** is one of the emblematic centres of the city with its statue of **General Espartero** at the center.

On the first Saturday before the 21st of September every year the **Fiesta de San Mateo**, wine festival takes place in the Paséo del Espolón is worth watching.

The **Plaza del Mercado** is a popular meeting place for the city's inhabitants.

Getting There & Back

To get there you should book a **flight to/from Bilboa, Pamplona or Madrid**

On arrival you may be interested in **hiring a car**, **book a train ticket** or **book a bus ticket** to take you to your final destination

Accommodation

Albergue Municipal,
Calle Rua Vieja 32.
T: (0034) 941 26 02 34
Beds: 90. Open all year round.
Has cooking & laundry facilities
as well as Internet access.

Albergue Juvenil, Calle
Caballero de la Rosa 38.
T: (0034) 941 29 11 45
Beds: 92. Open all year round.

Hostal La Cortijana **,
Beatos Mena y Navarrete 16.
T: (0034) 941 23 03 44 / 638 55
13 91
E: lacortijana@gmail.com
W: www.hostallacortijana.com

Pensión Cinco Villas,
Calle Labradores 21.
T: (0034) 655 97 85 75
W: www.infohostal.com

Pensión El Ensueño *,
Avenida. de Burgos 100.
T: (0034) 605 89 36 20 / 655 860
829

Pensión Elvira IV *, Calle María
Teresa Gil de Gárate 20-22.
T: (0034) 941 24 01 50

Pensión Florida *,
Calle Trinidad 6.
T: (0034) 941 22 12 35

Hostal Residencia Meson Pepa
**, Avda. de Aragón 9.
T: (0034) 941 234 011

Hostal Residencia Rioja
Condestable **,
Calle Doctores Castroviejo 5.
T: (0034) 941 24 72 88
E: hosrioja@fer.es

Hotel Isasa **,
Calle Doctores Castroviejo 13.
T: (0034) 941 25 65 99
E: hotelisasa@infonegocio.com

Camping La Playa,
Avda. de la Playa 6-8.
T: (0034) 941 25 22 53
E: info@campinglaplaya.com
W: www.campinglaplaya.com

Where to Eat

Calle Laurel, known as "the path of the elephants" and **Calle San Juan** are typical streets where various restaurants and tapas-bars offer the best *pinchos* and *tapas* in northern Spain. In its bars you can find all kinds of typical dishes, such as stuffed & grilled mushrooms, stuffed peppers and roast pepperoni.

Calle Portales is the main street in the old town, where people like to walk and sit in the terraces to have a meal or good wine.

Asparagus, beans, peppers, artichokes and other vegetables and pulses are the basic ingredients of a long list of traditional dishes such as vegetable stew, potatoes 'la riojana', and lamb and kid cutlets with vine shoots or stuffed peppers.

The traditional desserts are pears in wine, almond pastries from Arnedo or the marzipan from Soto.

Tourist Information/ Oficina de Turismo

Tourist Office, Paseo del Espolón, Principe de Vergara 1.
T: (0034) 941 29 12 60 / 902 27 72 00
E: info@lariojaturismo.com
W: www.lariojaturismo.com

Municipal Tourist Office, Calle Portales 50.
T: (0034) 941 27 33 53
E: infoturismo@logrono.org
W: www.lariojaturismo.com
Opening: Mon–Sat 10:00–14.00 & 16:30–19:30; Sun 10:00–14.00 Jul - Sep and National Festivals from 9:00 to 14:00 & 17:00 to 20:00

Post Office / Oficina de Correos

Main Post Office, Avenida General Vives 1.
T: (0034) 987 410 928
Opening: Mon - Fri 08:30 - 20:30
Saturday: 09:30 - 13:00

Others

Train Station: Plaza de Europa.
T: (0034) 902 240 202

Bus Station:
Avenida de España 1.
T: (0034) 941 235 983

Airport: Carretera LO-20.
T: (0034) 941 277 400

Stage 8: Logroño - Nájera
Map 2: Page 242 | Distance: 29.5km

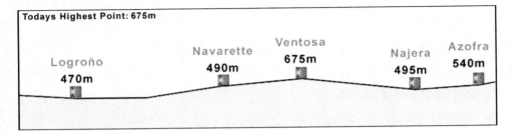

 Logroño

633.5km to Santiago |
Altitude: 470m | Population:
148,000

Head out of Logroño along Calle Rúa Vieja onto Calle Barriocepo, passing the Iglesia de Santiago and the 16th century pilgrim fountain **Fuente de los Peregrinos**.

Beside this is a square with a mosaic of the game Juego de la Oca. This is a snakes and ladders style game and the board and pieces represent the pilgrimage to Santiago.

Continue on through the Old Town, Casco Antiguo, until you come to Plaza del Parlemento. Continue through the **Puerta del Camino** in Logroño's town walls.

Head out through the suburbs of Logroño keeping an eye for the yellow arrow way markers. Go straight along the Marqués de Murrieta over the railway line to Avenida Burgos then turn left onto Calle Portillejo. For the next few kilometres you'll walk through open parkland along a paved track to **Plantano de la Grajera**.

Take a right along the reservoir wall, over a footbridge to the picnic area, cafe and fountain.

Follow the gravel track around the lake passing a fountain and head uphill along an a path that runs parallel to the main road where pilgrims have placed hundreds of small wooden crosses in the wire fence on the right.

At the end of the fence, cross the main road onto a dirt track through fields and vineyards crossing the motorway over a footbridge.

You now come to the ruins of a 12th century mediaeval **Hospital de San Juan de Acre, which** as founded to look after pilgrims walking the Camino.

Continue on, climbing some steep steps over a bypass and into the town of **Navarette**.

 Navarette

A H A ⑪ ◉ € i ⛟ ✚ @

621km to Santiago | Altitude: 490m | Population: 2500

Information

Navarette is an historic hillside town with a population of around 2,500.

Near the top of the town you'll

find the 16th century **Iglesia de la Asunción,** which has a very impressive Baroque altarpiece.

Other buildings to look out for include the **Ermita de Santa Maria del Buen Suceso** and the **Castillo**, which is on the highest part of the *Cerro Tedeón* and has great views of the surrounding countryside. You'll find a square with cafés and restaurants at the lower part of the town near the main road.

Tourist Office (Summer only), Calle Cuesta el Caño.
T: (0034) 941 44 01 69

Tourist Office, Paseo del Espolón, Principe de Vergara, 1.
T: (0034) 941 29 12 60 / 902 27 72 00
E: info@lariojaturismo.com
W: www.lariojaturismo.com

Accommodation

Albergue Municipal, Calle San Juan.
T: (0034) 941 44 07 76
Beds: 40. Open all year round. Has cooking & laundry facilities.

Albergue El Cántaro, Calle Herrerías 16.
T: (0034) 941 44 11 80
Beds: 22. Open all year round and has laundry facilities. Have hostel rooms available.

Camping Navarette, Carrettera Navarrete-Entrena.
T: (0034) 941 44 01 69
E: campingnavarrete@fer.es
W: www.campinglarioja.com

Hostal La Carioca *, Calle Prudencio Muñoz 1.
T: (0034) 941 44 08 05 / 941 44 00 06

Hostal Villa de Navarette *, Cale la Cruz 2.
T: (0034) 941 44 03 18
E: reservas@hostalvilladenavarrete.com
W: www.hostalvilladenavarrete.com

Leaving Navarette, take a right up the Calle La Cruz to the church square and the **Iglesia de la Ascunción**. Turn left down the Calle Mayor Alta onto the main road passing the cemetery.

The 13th century gateway was brought here from the **Hospital de San Juan de Acre**. The capitals show various battle scenes including the battle between Roldán and the giant Ferragut. Pass the cemetery along a right red earth track; this red clay soil is used by local potters, through vineyards running parallel to the main road.

Continue on over the Río de la Fuente and crossing the road to Sotés at the Vitivinicola Wine co-operative. You can take a left here to the Albergue Bodegas Fernando J Rodrigues in **Sotes**

 # Sotes

Accommodation

Albergue Bodegas Fernando J Rodrigues.
T: (0034) 670 05 32 29
Beds: 18. Open May - Oct.
Has laundry facilities.

Or you can continue on the track that runs alongside the main road. After a few kilometres the path leaves the road on towards the village of **Ventosa**

 # Ventosa

613.5km to Santiago | Altitude: 675m | Population: 150

Information

With a population of around 150 Ventosa's main monument is the 16th century **Iglesia de San Saturnino Siglo**.

In the first weekend of July the locals hold the **Fiesta de La Virgen Blanca**.

Tourist Office, Paseo del Espolón, Principe de Vergara 1.
T: (0034) 941 29 12 60 / 902 27 72 00
E: info@lariojaturismo.com
W: www.lariojaturismo.com

Accommodation

Albergue de San Saturnio, Just below the church.
T: (0034) 941 44 18 99
Beds: 50. Open all year round. Has cooking & laundry facilities.

Leaving Ventosa head uphill on dirt track through countryside passing small piles of stone mounds left by pilgrims over the years.

Keep going uphill towards Alto de San Antón. On your right you can see the ruins of the **Convento de San Antón**, you also get views of Nájera.

Continue on on the red dirt track trough vineyards until you cross the main road to the right of the Poyo de Roldán, Mound of Roland.

This is the spot where Roland is alleged to have killed the giant Ferragut and then freed the Christian Knights of Charlemagne's Army from captivity.

Carry on on the track across a main road then across footbridge over the Río Yalde continuing around the side of a gravel factory, through a vineyard towards the outskirts of Nájera. Follow the signs for the town centre passing the Guardia Civil and the **Convento de Santa Helena**. Cross the bridge over the Río Najerilla taking a left on the other side to the albergue municipal in **Nájera**

 Nájera

🅰 🅷 🄰 🍴 🗑 € 𝒊 🛒 ➕ @

604km to Santiago | Altitude: 495m | Population: 7200

Information

In the 11th century King Sancho III, modified the camino route so that Nájera became a resting place for pilgrims.

The town is divided by the river Najerilla and the **Monasterio de Santa María La Real** stands on its banks. Built in 1032, it underwent a number of modifications in the 15th century.

It's **Royal Pantheon**, bears the tombs of some thirty monarchs including the mausoleum of the Dukes of Nájera and, in the crypt, the cave where according to legend the Virigin appeared before King Don García, who then ordered the construction on the site. Facing the monastery is the **Nájera History and Archaeological Museum**, with sections on prehistory, the Romans, the medieval period, ethnography and painting, as well as material from the Nájera region.

Also of interest is the **Iglesia de Santa Cruz** situated in Plaza de San Miguel. If you are staying in Nájera you'll find a selection of bars and cafés in Plaza de España and Plaza de Navarra. If you want to do a bit of shopping you should head for the Calle Mayor.

Tourist Information,
Plaza San Miguel 10.
T: (0034) 941 36 00 41
E: najera@lariojaturismo.com
W: www.aytonajera.es

Accommodation

Albergue Municipal,
Plaza del Mercado.
Beds: 93. Open all year round.
Has cooking & laundry facilities.

Alergue Sancho III,
Calle San Marcial 6.
T: (0034) 941 36 11 38
Beds: 10. Open Apr - Oct. Offers pilgrim menu in the downstairs restaurant.

Camping El Rueda, Carretera Logroño-Burgos-Vigo-Nájera-Ciudad.
T: (0034) 941 36 01 02

Hostal Cepa *, Cepa 2.

T: (0034) 941 36 29 57

E: hispanonajera@yahoo.es

Hostal Ciudad de Nájera,

Calleja San Miguel 14.

T: (0034) 941 36 06 60

E: info@ciudaddenajera.com

W: www.ciudaddemajera.com

Hotel San Fernando **,

San Julian 1.

T: (0034) 941 36 37 00

E: sanfernando@sanmillan.com

W: www.sanmillan.com

Hotel Duques de Nájera,

El Carmén 7.

T: (0034) 941 41 04 21

E:

info@hotelduquesdenajera.com

Stage 9: Nájera - Santo Domingo de la Calzada
Map 2: Page 242 | Distance: 21km

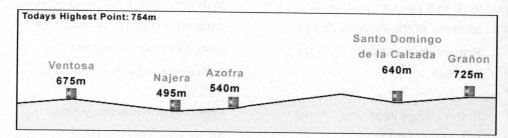

 ## Nájera

604km to Santiago |
Altitude: 495m | Population:
7200

Information

Leave Nájera through the Plaza
de Navarre past the **Eglesia de
Santa María Real** and then past
the frontón. Continue into the
zona natural on the red dirt
tracks. After a few kilometres
you'll reach a high point where
you will be able to see the village
of Azofra. Continue on the way
marked track into **Azofra.**

 ## Azofra

598km to Santiago |
Altitude: 540m | Population:
300

Information

Azofra was the site of several
pilgrim hospitals in mediaeval
times and now has a population
of around 300 people. You'll find
the **Iglesia de Nuestra Señora
de Los Angeles** here which has
a carved statue Santiago
Peregrino inside.

On the outskirts of the village
you'll also find a park dedicated

to Virgen de Valbanera, the patroness of La Rioja. Across from this you can see what remains of the **Fuente de los Romeros**, a mediaeval pilgrim fountain.

In the village itself you'll find a few shops and bars.

Accommodation

Albergue Municipal, Calle Las Parras.
T: (0034) 941 37 90 49
Beds: 60 (in rooms of 2). Open all year round. Has cooking & laundry facilities as well as Internet access.

Albergue La Fuente. Near the fountain.
Beds: 12. Open May - Oct. Has cooking & laundry facilities.

Albergue. Beside Iglesia de Nuestra Señora de Los Angeles.
T: (0034) 941 37 90 57
Beds: 26. Open all year.

Leave Azofra though the village park passing the shrine to the Virgen de Valbanera and the fountain. Take a left onto a track passing a medaeival road sign, rollo, marking the border between Azofra & Alescanco.

From here follow the yellow arrow way markers through fields then climbing up to the Rioja Alta Golf Club. Continue on into the village of **Cirueña**.

Continue through Cirueña on the main route on farm tracks until you reach the outskirts of **Santo Domingo de la Calzada.**

The track passes some factories before joining the main road. Follow this road to the crossing into the old town walking down the Calle Mayor, which takes you to the albergue and the cathedral.

Santo Domingo de la Calzada

583km to Santiago | Altitude: 640m | Population: 5600

Information

Santo Domingo de la Calzada's mediaeval streets were declared a National Historic Interest Site and are home to some grand buildings and plazas, particularly its walls, the **Catedral Santo Domingo de la Calzada** and the old Pilgrims' Hospital.

Santo Domingo founded the town in 1044 to help the pilgrims who travelled to Santiago de Compostela. It was here that he built a bridge, a shelter, a hospital and a hermitage, the origin of the town and city (a title awarded by Alfonso XI in 1334).

The cathedral is located in the central Plaza del Santo, was built in 1158 in the Gothic style, although it has elements of Romanesque origin, such as its main front and apse, and others, which are Baroque or Renaissance in style, such as the slim freestanding bell, tower.

You can climb to the top of the tower where you get gret views of the town and the bell tower. There is also the chicken coup at the rear of the cathedral, which is home to a cock and a hen. This was built to serve as a reminder of a miracle, which took place here when a roast cock and a hen were miraculously revived proving the innocence of a young man who had been wrongfully hanged but survived his sentence.

The old pilgrims hospital next to the cathedral, originally built by Santo Domingo has now been converted into an impressive luxury Parador. Pedro I "The

Cruel" built the walls, which fortify its medieval layout. The houses on the Calle Mayor, the **City Hall** and the **Convento de San Francisco** are also major points of interest. The **Casa de Santos**, a Pilgrim's Information Office, is also worth a visit.

The town has a large variety of shops, bars & restaurants, which can be found along the Calle Mayor and the Paseo.

Tourist Office, Calle Mayor, 70.
T: (0034) 941 34 12 30
E:santodomingo@lariojaturismo.org

W:
www.santodomingodelacalzada.org

Accommodation

Albergue Municipal Casa de la Confradía del Santo,
Calle Mayor 42.
T: (0034) 941 34 33 90
Beds: 84 in four rooms.

Overflow in ground floor dormitory. Open all year. Has cooking facilities.

Albergue Abadía Cisterciense Nuestra Señora de la Anunciación, Calle Mayor 29.
T: (0034) 941 34 05 70
Beds: 34 beds in 6 rooms. Open May - Sep. Has cooking & laundry faciities.

Hospedería Santa Teresita *,
Calle Pinar 2.
T: (0034) 941 34 07 00

Pensión Albert *,
Calle Beato Hermosilla 20.
T: (0034) 941 34 08 27

Pensión El Peregrino *,
Avenida de Calahorra.
T: (0034) 941 34 21 28

Pensión Miguel *,
Calle Juan Carlos I 23.
T: (0034) 941 34 32 52

Hotel El Corregidor **, Mayor
14-15. Tel: (0034) 941 34 21 28

**Parador Esc. de Sto. Domingo
Bernardo de Fresneda ***,**

Plaza Pl. San Francisco 1.
T: (00340 941 34 11 50
E:
bernardodefresneda@parador.e
s
W: www.parador.es

**Parador de Santo Domindo de
la Calzada ***,**
Plaza El Santo, 3.
T: (0034) 941 34 03 00
E: sto.domingo@parador.es
W: www.parador.es

Stage 10: St Domingo de la Calzada - Belorado

Map 2: Page 242 | Distance: 24km

Todays Highest Point: 792m						
Santo Domingo de la Calzada		Redecilla del Camino	Villamayor del Rio	Belorado		Tosantos
640m	Grañon 725m	738m	787m	770m		820m

Santo Domingo de la Calzada

583km to Santiago | Altitude: 640m | Population: 5600

Leaving Santo Domingo de la Calzada, pass the cathedral and onto the Calle Mayor and onto the main road. You come to the Puente del Santo, Saint's Bridge, and Santo Domingo's original bridge.

Cross over the Río Oja, then across the road onto broad tracks. Keep going until you come to a junction where a sign offers you the choice between a longer route (3km) to the left through fields and a shorter route (2km) to the right along the road.

The longer route is the more pleasant of the two. Taking the left through farmland and pass a cemetery and another small Ermita, keep straight on until you enter **Grañon**

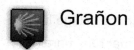 # Grañon

574km to Santiago |
Altitude: 725m

Information

Grañon is a walled town that
once had two monasteries and a
pilgrim hospice. Today it's main
building is the recently restored
Iglesia de San Juan Bautista,
which has been built over the
site of an old monastery

Accommodation

**Albergue Hospital de
Peregrinos**, next to the **Iglesia
de San Juan Bautista.**
Beds: 40. Open all year. Has
cooking facilities.

Casa Jacobeo **,
Calle Mayor 32.
T: (0034) 941 42 06 84

Heading out of the village, take a
left continue on a track then turn
right across a stream before

taking another left up to a sign
indicating that you are about to
leave the region of La Rioja and
into the region of Castilla y Léon.
Keep on for another 2 - 3 km
until you reach the village of
Redicilla del Camino.

Redicilla del Camino

 570km to Santiago |
Altitude: 738m

Information

Redicillo del Camino is a small
village where you'll find the
**Iglesia de Nuestra Señora de
la Calle,** inside you'll find a
beautiful Romanesque font. The
albergue is built on the site of the
mediaeval pilgrim hospice,
Hospitla de San Lázar.

Accommodation

Albergue San Lázaro,
Calle Mayor 32.
T: (0034) 947 58 02 83
Beds: 50 in 4 rooms. Open all
year. Has cooking facilities.

Continue on between the church and the albergue along the Calle Mayor. Cross the main road and then take the track until you arrive at **Castildelgado.**

Castildelgado

568km to Santiago | Altitude: 753m

Information

Castildelgado was once home to a monastery and a pilgrim's hospice. The Iglesia de San Pedro has seen better days, and beside this you can see the ruins of the Casa de Berberana and the pilgrims hospice which was founded by Alfonso VII.

There is a bar / Restaurant in the village as well a panaderia and a hostal.

Accommodation

Hostal Chocolatero **, on the main road.
T: (0034) 947 58 80 6

Head through the village back onto a track that runs parallel to the main road. After 1km take a left onto a smaller road and continue on until you reach **Viloria de la Rioja.**

Viloria de la Rioja

566km to Santiago | Altitude: 787m

Information

Viloria de la Rioja is the birthplace of Santo Domingo. The house in which he was born was recently demolished and the font in which he was baptised has been removed from the old church.

Accommodation

Albergue Acacio y Orietta,
Calle Nueva 6.
T: (0034) 947 58 52 20.
Beds: 12. Open all year. Has cooking, dining & laundry facilities.

Head out of the village on a quiet country road and after 1km take the track alongside the main road until you reach **Villamayor del Río**.

 # Villamayor del Río

563km to Santiago |
Altitude: 787m

Information

There is not much to Villamayor del Río. There is a restaurant on the main road, but if you do intend on going in be sure to leave your backpack and walking sticks outside, it's a little posh.

Accommodation

Albergue San Luis de Francia,
on road to Quintanilla del Monte.
Tel: (0034) 947 58 05 66.
Beds: 52 in 9 rooms. Open all year. Offers dinner & breakfast.

Continue on the track parallel to the main road until you come to a picnic / rest area, cross over and follow the track into **Belorado**.

 # Belorado

559km to Santiago |
Altitude: 770m | Population: 2,100

Information

The relaxed town Belorado lies in the valley of the Río Tirón in the shadow of the mountain with its castle and the ruins of a medaeival fortress.

The 16th century **Iglesia de Santa María** can be found next to the albergue and has some impressive altars, some depicting Santiago Matamoros y Peregino. Behind the church you can still see the caves that were once home to hermits, including

San Capraiso. You can also see the 18th Century **Iglesia de San Pedro** in the Plaza Mayor.

The **Monasterio de Santa María de la Bretonera**, which was re-established in the 14th century, can be found on the outskirts of the town.The Plaza Mayor is lined with restaurants, shops & bars.

Tourist Information,
Town Hall, Plaza Mayor.
T: (0034) 947 58 02 26.

Accommodation

Albergue Parroquial, Calle Corro, Next to Iglesia de Santa María.
Beds: 30. Open all year. Has cooking facilities.

Albergue A Santiago, as you head into Belorado.
T: (0034) 947 56 21 64.
Beds: 110. Open Apr - Oct. Has cooking, dining & laundry facilities as well as Internet access and small swimming pool.

Albergue El Corro,
Calle Mayor/Calle El Corro.
T: (0034) 670 69 11 73
Beds: 40. Open all year round. Has cooking facilities.

Albergue Cuatro Cantones,
Calle Hipólito Lopez Bernal 10.
T: (0034) 696 42 77 07
Beds: 60. Open all year round. Has cooking & laundry facilities.

Albergue El Caminante,
Calle Mayor 36.
T: (0034) 947 58 02 31
Beds: 22. Open Apr - Oct. Had
cooking & laundry facilities as
well as Internet access.

Pension Ojarre,
Calle Santiago 16
T: (0034) 947 58 02 23

Pension Toni,
Calle Redecilla del Campo 7
T: (0034) 947 58 05 25

Hotel Belorado *,
Avenida Generalismo 30
T: (0034) 947 58 06 84

Hotel Jacobeo **, Avenida
Generalismo 3 Tel: (0034) 947
58 07 26

Stage 11: Belorado - San Juan de Ortega
Map 3: Page 243 | Distance: 23km

 **Belorado**

559km to Santiago |
Altitude: 770m | Population:
2,100

Leave Belorado through the
Plaza Mayor taking a left onto
the Calle Hipolito Lopez Bernal.

Head through the suburbs of
Belorado passing the Convento
de Santa Clara.Cross the main
road and then cross the Río
Tirón via a wooden
footbridge.Take the path that
runs parallel to the main road
passing a picnic / rest area into

the hamlet of **Tosantos**.

Tosantos

 555km to Santiago |
Altitude: 820m

Information

You'll find the Bar El Castaño on
the main road.

Accommodation

**Albergue San Francisco de
Asís**, Calle Santa Maria.
T: (0034) 947 58 00 85
Beds: 30. Open all year round.
Has dining facilities.

Head out of Tosantos along a dirt track. On the way you'll pass the 12th century **Ermita de Nuestra Señora de Pena,** which is built into the cliff. Continue on

this track until you reach the hamlet of **Villambistia**.

Villambistia

553km to Santiago | Altitude: 865m

Information

It is an old tradition in the village that passing pilgrims refresh themselves by completely immersing their heads in the village fountain. This is optional of course.

Local monuments include the

17th century **Iglesia de San Esteban Protomártir** and the **Ermita de San Roque**. In August the 14th to the 16th the village holds the Fiesta de Nuestra Señora and San Roque.

Accommodation

Albergue San Roque, in the centre of Villambistia.
T: (0034) 947 58 21 47
Beds: 27. Open during summer months. Has cooking & laundry facilities. Cross over a stream on the way out of the village and on into **Espinosa del Camino**.

 # Espinosa del Camino

551km to Santiago | Altitude: 895m

Accommodation

Albergue La Campaña.
T: (0034) 678 47 93 61
Beds: 10 in two rooms. Opens Feb - Dec. Has dining facilities.

Pass through Espinosa del Camino onto a dirt track to the top of a hill. You will be able to see Villafranca Montes de Oca from here. Continuing down the other side passing the 9th century ruins of the **Monasterio San Felices de Oca**. The remains of Diego Porcelos, who founded Burgos, are buried underneath the ruins.

Continue on the track, which goes on to meet with the main road leading over the Río Oca into **Villafranca de Montes de Oca**

Villafranca de Montes de Oca

548km to Santiago | Altitude: 955m | Population: 200

Information

Villafranca de Montes de Oca is located in a valley at the foot of the Montes de Oca, which was once notorious for bandits and robbers.

The towns name is believed to come form an early Roman settlement, Auca, which was once situated here.

Whilst here you should try to visit the 18th century **Iglesia de Santiago Apóstol**. Inside you'll find a Baroque statue of Saint James and a font made from a giant scallop shell, which originated in the Philippines.

There's also the 14th century **Hospital de Peregrinos de San Antón Abad** (also known as **Hospital de la Reina**), which was built, at the command of Doña Juana, wife of King

Enrique II. It has now been converted into an albergue. Other monuments include the 8th century **Ermita de Nuestra Señora de Oca.**

On the outskirts of Villafranca is a natural reserve where you'll find a large fountain, which according to legend began to flow at the site on which San Indalecio, a disciple of San Jacques, was martyred.

Accommodation

Albergue Municipal,
Calle Mayor.
T: (0034) 947 58 21 24
Beds: 36 in two dormitories. Open all year. Has cooking facilities.

Albergue San Antón Abad,
Next to the Hotel San Antón Abad.
Beds: 12. Open all year. Has cooking & laundry facilities.

Hostal El Pájaro **.
Calle Mayor.
T: (0034) 94758 20 29

In Villafranca take a right off the main road passing the Iglesia de Santiago Apóstol. Climb up through a oak and pine wooded area to the Fuente de Mojapán.

Continue on the tree-lined path climbing until you reach the **Monumentos de los Caidos**, a memorial to the victims of the Spanish Civil war.

From this point descend to a footbridge over a stream along the track and head on until you come to the **Ermita de la Valdefuentes**. From here climb up a little more before descending into the small hamlet of **San Juan de Ortega.**

San Juan de Ortega

536km to Santiago |
Altitude: 1010m |
Population: 200

Information

San Juan was a disciple of San Domingo, and just like San Domingo he built bridges, hospices, hotels & churches to help pilgrims throughout this region.

He also founded an order here and built the Iglesia de San Juan de Ortega. The church was later restored in the 15th century after falling into a state of disrepair.

The tomb of San Juan with its Gothic canopy over the Romanesque sarcophagus can be found in the crypt underneath the monastery church.

A pilgrimage to the church was supposedly the last hope for childless women. Queen Isabel la Católica visited the church in 1477 and had three children afterwards. As a sign of her gratitude she ordered the rebuilding of the chapel including a gift of the canopy above the Saint's tomb.

An architectural masterpiece is the **Milagros de la Luz**, Miracles of Light. In the late afternoon in the spring and autumn equinox a ray of sunlight illuminates the Virgin of the Annunciation. (21st March 6:00pm & 21st Sept 19:00)

Accommodation

Albergue, Parish Hostel.
T: (0034) 947 56 04 38
Beds: 58 in 3 rooms. Open all year.

Don José María used to serve garlic soup after evening pilgrim mass. The custom still goes on despite his death in 2008.

Stage 12: San Juan de Ortega - Burgos
Map 3: Page 243 | Distance: 26km

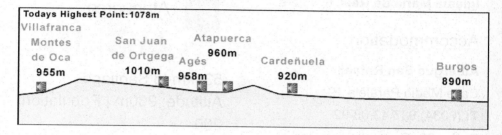

 ## San Juan de Ortega

536km to Santiago |
Altitude: 1010m |
Population: 200

Leaving San Juan de Ortega take the well-marked track on the right uphill through the pinewood forest of Monte de Oca.

The path levels out, you'll pass a

few large crosses on the way, and then head downhill into the village of **Agés**.

Agés

532.5km to Santiago |
Altitude: 958m

Information

The 16th century **Iglesia de Santa Eulalia** with it's elegant Baroque bell tower reign over the town of Agés.

The temple once contained the remains of King García de Navarre who was killed by his brother Fernando I de Castilla in 1054 in the famous battle of

Atepuerca.The remains now rest in the Pantéon Real in the **Iglesia María de Real** in Nájera.

Accommodation

Albergue San Rafael,
Calle Medio Paralela 19.
T: (0034) 947 43 03 92
Beds: 36. Open all year. Has a laundry facility as well as Internet access.

Albergue Casa Caracol,
Calle la Iglesia.
T: (0034) 947 43 04 13
Beds: 10 in a few rooms.

Albergue El Pajar de Agés,
Calle Medio Paralela 12.
T: (0034) 947 43 03 92
Beds: 38. Open all year. Has cooking, dining & laundry facilities as well as internet access.

Continue on through Agés crossing the Río Vena via a Romanesque bridge built by San Juan de Ortega. Follow the paved road for a couple of kilometres into **Atapuerca**

Atapuerca

530km to Santiago | Altitude: 960m | Population: 200

Information

The impressive Gothic & Renaissance style **Iglesia de San Martín** over looks Atapuerca from a small hill.

Atapuerca has recently become one of the most important archaeological sites in the world since the discovery in 1994 of 800,000 year old early human remains.

The excavation site is ongoing and has been declared a natural heritage site by UNESCO. Many of the findings are now on display in Burgos in the Museo de Burgos and some in the Museo de Ibeas in the village of Ibeas de Juarros near

Atapuerca. You can also arrange a visit of the site, which sits in a military area, from here or from Atapuerca. For more information visit www.visitasatapuerca.com

Tourist Information,
Centro de Interpretacíon.
T: (0034) 947 42 14 62

Accommodation

Albergue El Peregrino,
Calle Carretera 105.
T: (0034) 661 58 08 82
Beds: 36 in six rooms. Open all year. Has a kitchen facility.

Albergue La Hutte, near the parish church.
T: (0034) 947 43 03 20
Beds: 20. Has cooking & laundry facilities.

Hotel Papasol **, next to Albergue La Hutte.
T: (0034) 947 34 03 20

Alternatively you can continue 2.5km further along the route to the village of Olmos de Atapuerca.

Olmos de Atapuerca

Information
From here you can rejoin the camino by following the yellow arrow way markers onto a track up the Sierra de Atapuerca through oak woodland until you re join the camino route from Atapuerca.

Tourist Information,
Calle Encimera 10.
T: (0034) 947 26 49 66 / 699 27 38 56
E: info@casarrotalacampesina.com

Accommodation

Albergue Municipal,
Calle La Iglesia.
Beds: 32. Open from Easter - Nov. Has cooking facilities.

Hotel Casarrota La Campesina **, Calle Encimera 10.
T: (0034) 947 26 49 66.

From Atapuerca take a left and follow the track into the Sierra de Atapuercoa. Gradually climb onto the high Matagrande plain where you get great views of the City of Burgos.

Continue left of the TV / Radio towers following along the fence passed a quarry. Carry on until you reach a fork on the road.

Taking a left

Left takes you on a quiet route through the old hamlet of **Villalval** passing an ancient Roman well and into **Cardeñuela Riopico**.

Cardeñuela Riopico

526km to Santiago | Altitude: 920m

Accommodation

Albergue Municipal, behind the town hall.
T: (0034) 947 43 09 11
Beds: 16. Keys can be found in the town hall of in the Bar La Parada.

Continue on until you meet up with the other route leading into **Orbaneja Riopico.**

Head through Orbeneja, crossing the bridge over the main road and here you have another choice to make.

The recommended route into Burgos is on the left along a farm track thats runs alongside Burgos Airport, through wheat fields and then take the road into Castañares,

a quiet suburb of the City of Burgos. From here you can head on along the main road and the busy city traffic into Burgos.

A nicer alternative is to take the path that runs along the river. To take this route, cross the road to Camino Santa María Sendero, pass a park and though a small housing estate.

Head across a bridge passed a cement works and then the Campo del Futbol el Molinar complex.

Take the footbridge over the Río Arlanzón through the Parque Fuentes Blancas into the centre of **Burgos**.

Taking a right

Right is a less pleasant route, taking the road through the suburbs of the city. Cross a bridge over railway tracks into the modern industrial suburb of **Villafría**

 # Villafría

518km to Santiago | Altitude: 885m

Accommodation

Hotel Buenos Aires **.
T: (0034) 947 48 37 70

Hotel Las Vegas **.
T: (0034) 947 48 44 53

Hotel Iruñako.
T: (0034) 947 48 41 26

There is also a bus service (Number 8) into the center of Burgos for those who want to avoid the traffic. Continue along the main road passing the industrial estate onto Calle Vitoria.

Take a left after the Guardia Civil building, then another left at the Centro Comercial Camino de la Plata onto the Calle Las

Calzadas, which will take you into **Burgos**.

 Burgos

🅐 🅗 ⛺ 🍴 ☕ € ℹ️ 🛒 ➕

510km to Santiago | Altitude: 890m | Population: 170,000

Information

Burgos is the capital of the province of Burgos and has a population of around 178,000 with another 15,000 or so in it's suburbs. It sits at 884 metres above sea level, and it does get quite cold in the winter months.

As you come into the city via the **Puente de Santa María** you'll come to the **Arco de Santa María**, an impressive gateway carved with statues of different local dignitaries. Pass through the gateway into the Plaza Del Rey San Fernando, home of Spain's finest Gothic Cathedral that completely dominates the centre of the old town. Work begun on the cathedral in 1221, and construction took only 22 years, but it was added to over the following couple of centuries. UNESCO declared it a World Heritage Site in 1984.

Towers terminating in octagonal spires covered with open stonework traceries flank the west front. The middle section, which serves for an entrance, has three alabaster pilasters, the intercolumnar spaces bearing panel-pictures representing the martyrdom of saints.

Inside there is a huge amount of sculptures and artwork. The Capilla de Santa Tecla is home to Burgos' famous 15th century clock, the **Papamoscas**. The main bridge into the city is the **Puente de San Pablo**, where you'll find a statue, which commemorates the city's hero, El Cid. Other sites worth a visit are the Monasterio de Las Huelgas on the outskirts of the city, which was founded in 1180 by King Alfonso VIII, and was begun in a pre-Gothic style, although almost every style has been introduced over the years.

To the East of the city you'll find the **Cartuja de Miraflores**, a Carthusian monastery founded in the 15th century. The church includes the mausoleum of Juan II and of his wife Isabel de Portugal. The multicoloured altarpiece is by Gil de Siloé, and is supposedly gilded with the first ever gold brought back from the New World.

There's also the **Iglesia de San Lorenzo**, with it's impressive Baroque ceiling, the **Iglesia de San Esteban** with it's museum of altarpieces and the **Iglesia de Santa Áqueda** where El Cid made Algonso VI swear that he had nothing to do with the murder of his brother Sancho II. The Museo de Burgos is found across the river in the Casa

History

Founded in 884, Burgos has played a significant political and military role in the history of Spain. It was the capital of Castilla y León from 1073 until it lost the honour to Valladolid in 1492.

Until well into the 17th century Burgos' wealth came from it's wool exports. It used this wealth to finance most of the architecture seen in the city today. Franco made Burgos his headquarters during the civil war and the industrial development he helped bring about in the 1950s and 1960s brought wealth to the city.

Layout

The center of the old town of Burgos is dominated by the Gothic cathedral and sits between the Río Arlanzón and the hill behind where you can still see what remains of the town's old castle.

Across the Puente de Santa María into the new town along Calle Madrid you'll find the bus station on the right and take a left along the Calle de la Merced then left onto Avenida Conde de Guadalhorce to the train station.

You'll find some budget accommodation on this side of the bridge. If it's a hot day and you fancy an ice cream I recommend the ice cream shop on the left-hand side of Calle de La Paloma which runs from Plaza del Rey Fernando down the side of the Cathedral.

Getting There & Back

To get there you should book a **flight to/from Bilboa, Madrid or Valladolid**

Accommodation

Albergue Municipal Casa del Cubo, Calle Fernán Gonzalez 28.
T: (0034) 947 46 09 22
Beds: 76. Open all year. Has cooking & laundry facilities as well as Internet access.

Albergue Divina Pastora, Calle Laín Calvo 10.
T: (0034) 947 20 79 52
Beds: 18. Open all year round.

Albergue Juvenil Gil de Siloé, Avenida de Cantabria.
T: (0034) 947 22 02 77
Beds: 110. Open all year.

Hotel El Jacabeo **, Calle San Juan.
T: (0034) 947 26 01 02
E: hoteljacobeo@hoteljacobeo.com
W: www.hoteljacobeo.com

Hotel Norte y Londres **, Plaza Alonso Martinez 10.
T: (0034) 947 26 41 25
E: info@hotelnorteylondres.com
W: www.hotelnorteylondres.com

Hotel Mesón Del Cid,
Calle Fernán González 29.
T: (0034) 947 20 87 15
E:mesondelcid@mesondelcid.es
W: www.mesondelcid.es

Camping Fuentes Blancas,
Carretera Burgos - Cartuja de
Miraflores 3km.
T: (0034) 947 48 60 16
E: info@campingburgos.com
W: www.campingburgos.com

Check:
http://tinyurl.com/hotels-burgos

Where to Eat

The most famous food of Burgos
is without doubt it's fresh cheese
with slight goat-milk-flavor, called
Queso de Burgos. It is
extremely popular not only here
but also in most other regions of
Spain. Burgos' cuisine has a high
reputation for a variety of other
recipes such as roasted lamb,
chopped pork, blood pudding,
red beans (called Ibeas) and
hotpot. There are excellent fish-
dishes as well, river crab salad
and codfish á la Burgalesa are
amongst the specialties of this
region.

Local meal times are generally
14:00 - 15:00 for lunch and 21:00
- 22.30 for dinner.

Tourist Information/
Oficina de Turismo

Tourist Information, Plaza
Alonso Martínez 7.
T: (0034) 947 20 31 25
E: info@turismoburgos.org
W: www.turismoburgos.org
Opening: Mon - Fri 10:00 - 14:00
& 17:00 - 19:00 Sat 10:00am -
14:00

Also on the Calle de la Asunción
de Nuestra Señora 3. Open

every day from 10:30 - 14:00 &
16:00 - 20:00 Sun 10:30am -
14:00

Post Office / Oficina de Correos

Main Post Office, Plaza del
Conde de Castro.
T: (0034) 947 26 27 50
Opening hours: Mon - Fri
08:00am - 20:30 Sat 09:30am -
14:00

Medical & Emergency Services

**Emergency Number for all
services: 112**

General Hoapital Yague:
Avenida del Cid Campeador
T: (0034) 947 28 18 00

Stage 13: Burgos - Hontanas
Map 3: Page 243 | Distance: 31km

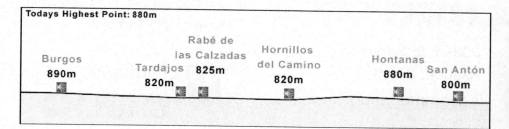

Todays Highest Point: 880m

Burgos 890m	Tardajos 820m	Rabé de las Calzadas 825m	Hornillos del Camino 820m

Hontanas 880m   San Antón 800m

 Burgos

510km to Santiago | Altitude: 890m | Population: 170,000

From Burgos follow the yellow arrow way markers onto Calle Emperador to the Iglesia de San Pedro de la Fuente and the Albergue Monasterio de San José.

Take a left to cross the Río Alrlanzón over the Puente de Malatos and cross the road by the Hospital Militar and on into the Parque Parral, passing the

Albergue on the left. At the other side of the park continue on before turning left at the Hotel Puerta Romeros and past a university campus before crossing the main road. Follow the route along the road and then onto a track passed a jail on your right that was once used to hold political prisoners during Franco's rule. Go straight on from here into **Villalbilla de Burgos**.

Villalbilla de Burgos

506km to Santiago |
Altitude: 840m

Accommodation

Albergue Municipal, behind the town hall.
T: (0034) 947 43 09 11
Beds: 16. Keys can be found in the town hall of in the Bar La Parada.

Heading through Villalbilla de Burgos and onto the track and cross over the Río Arlanzón via the Puente del Arzobispo. Take a left and pass under the railway,

follow along the main road for a while, then under the motorway passing the site of an old pilgrim hospice into **Tardajos**.

Tardajos

502.5km to Santiago |
Altitude: 820m

Information

The village of Tardajos is home to the **Iglesia de Nuestra Señora de la Asunción**. It also has a couple of bars and a shop on the main road

Accommodation

Albergue Municipal,
Calle Asunción.
T: (0034) 947 45 11 89
Beds: 20. Open all year.

Bar Ruiz *.
T: (0034) 947 45 11 25

Continue through Tardajos past a fountain in a small plaza and onto a quiet track over the Río Urbel and into **Rabé de las Calzadas**.

Rabé de las Calzadas

500km to Santiago | Altitude: 825m

Information

Rabé de las Calzadas is a small village with a population of around 150. It is home to the 13th century **Iglesia de Santa Mariña** and on the outskirts of the village you will find the **Ermita de Nuestra Señora de Monasterio**

Accommodation

Albergue Hospital de Peregrinos Santa Marina y Santiago,
Plaza Francisco Ribera 6.
T: (0034) 607 97 19 19
Beds: 50. Open Apr - Nov. Has dining facilities.

Albergue Libéranos Dómine.
Plaza Francisco Ribera.
T: (0034) 629 92 05 01
Beds: 25

Head out past the Ermita de Nuestra Señora de Monasterio and onto the *meseta*,the high plains of Central Spain.

Follow the track through fields and along streams to a resting spot beside the **Fuente de Praotorre**.

Continue through the way marked open landscape of cereal fields. After a few kilometres descend down the steep Cuesta Matamulos,

Mule Killer Slope. Cross the road and following the Río

Hormazuela into **Hornillos del Camino**

Hornillos del Camino

492km to Santiago |
Altitude: 820m

Information

Hornillos del Camino's Gothic **Iglesia de San Román** in the Plaza de la Iglesia is built on the site of an ancient military camp.

Next to it is the Fuente del Gallo and the albergue.

There is a small shop and bar along the main street.

Accommodation

Albergue Municipal,
Plaza de la Iglesia.
T: (0034) 947 47 12 20
Beds: 32 in three rooms. Open all year. Has a kitchen facility.

Casa Rural Sol a Sol **, Village entrance next to the shop. Tel: (0034) 649 87 60 91

Leave Hornillos del Camino alon the Calle Real, heading right at the end efore heading up onto the meseta again. Continue on for 5km and descend into the next valley and into **Arroyo San Bol**.

Arroyo San Bol

Information

There's a natural spring here and it is claimed that pilgrims who relieve their aching feet in the water will have no further foot problems from here to Santiago.

The spring is on the site of the former hamlet of San Boal which was deserted by its inhabitants for reasons unknown in 1503.

Accommodation

Albergue Municipal.
T: (0034) 947 16 10 53
Beds: 12. Open May - Oct. Has kitchen facilities.

Climb out of the San Bol valley and back out onto the meseta. After a few kilometres of walking along this long flat stretch of the camino you will catch sight of Hontanas tucked in a valley in the distance.

Continue on until the track runs steeply downhill and on into the village of **Hontanas.**

Hontanas

479km to Santiago |
Altitude: 880m

Information

The pilgrim village of Hontanas in tucked into a valley and is dominated by the 14th century

Iglesia de la Inmaculada Concepción.

Accommodation

Albergue El Puntido, Calle La Iglesia 6.
T: (0034) 947 37 85 97
Beds: 30 in three rooms. Open Mar - Sept. Has dining & laundry facilities as well as Internet access. Also offers hostel rooms.

Albergue Municipal San Juan El Nuevo, in the Méson de los Franceses.
T: (0034) 947 37 70 21
Beds: 20 in 2 rooms. Open all year. Has cooking & laundry facilities.

When this albergue is full the following two are opened:

Albergue El Viaje, Town Hall.
Beds: 14 in two rooms

Albergue La Escuela, Old School House
Beds: 21 in one dormitory

Hostal Cesar Arnaiz *,
Calle La Portadilla.
T: (0034) 947 37 85 21

Hostal Fuente Strella **,
Calle Mayor. Open Mar – Oct.
T: (0034) 947 37 72 61

Stage 14: Hontanas - Boadilla del Camino
Map 3: Page 243 | Distance: 32.5

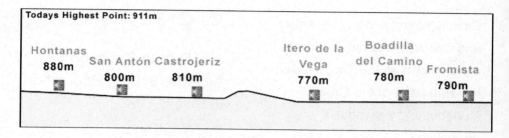

Todays Highest Point: 911m

Hontanas 880m | San Antón 800m | Castrojeriz 810m | Itero de la Vega 770m | Boadilla del Camino 780m | Fromista 790m

 Hontanas

479km to Santiago |
Altitude: 880m

Continue through Hontanas past a swimming pool and onto the path that runs along the bottom of a hillside. Walk past fields full of sunflowers before returning to the road.

The path more or less runs parallel to the road. Carry on past ruins of a mill and the abandoned village of San Miguel to the ruins of the Gothic **Convento de San Antón**. From here it's a short distance to and

San Antón

 San Antón

469.5km to Santiago |
Altitude: 800m

Information

Here the camino runs through the archway, Arco de San Antón, which once connected the monastery with the church. The monastery, which was built in the 12th century as a pilgrim hospital of the Orden de los Antonianos.

The Orden de los Antonianos were famous for their cure for Fuego de San Antón, St. Anthony's Fire, a fungal disease, similar in many ways to leprosy, which usually resulted in death.

Closely connected to San Antón and Castrojeriz is the 'T' shaped cross known as the Tau, which is the 19th letter of the Greek alphabet and a symbol of protection.

The monks of the Orden de San Antón wore it and gave it to pilgrims as protection against sickness and evil.

Accommodation

Albergue San Antón, inside the walls of the convent ruins.
T: (0034) 607 92 21 27
Beds: 12. Open May - Sept.

Passing through San Antón along the country road, Castrojeriz and the hill top ruins of it's 9th century castillo come into view. After a few kilometres you'll turn right passing the **Iglesia de Nuestra Señora del Manzano** and continue upwards into the centre of **Castrojeriz**

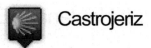 Castrojeriz

465.5km to Santiago | Altitude: 810m | Population: 970

Information

Castrojeriz, Castrum Sigerici, was founded by the Visigoths and was the scene of a lot of battles between the Moors and the Christians in the 9th & 10th century.

It was a royal residence in the 11th century and was a major stopping point along the camino boasting 8 pilgrim hospitals and 9 churches.

At the entrance of the village is the 13th century **Iglesia de Nuestra Señora del Manzano** where Santiago is reported to have seen an image of the Virgin in an apple tree and inside the church you can see a picture of Virgin del Manzano.

There is also the 16th century **Iglesia de Santo Domingo**, which is decorated with, carved skulls, in particular there are two of death's heads, O Mors, the past, & O Aeternitas, eternity. Inside you can see some exquisite 17th century tapestries.

Near the other side of the village is the 13th century **Iglesia de San Juan de los Caballeros**. Its impressive tower is a mix of Gothic and Romanesque styles and inside you'll find beautifully decorated Mudéjar ceilings.

For great views of the town and the surrounding countryside you should try to climb the hill up to the ruins of the 9th century castle. You'll see a number of bodegas scattered around the hillside.

Tourist Information, Calle Cordón 4, Tel: (0034) 947 37 70 01

Accommodation

Albergue El Refugio Tradicional San Juan, Calle Cordón.
T: (0034) 947 37 74 00
Beds: 28 in two dormitories. Open all year.

Albergue Municipal San Estaban, Plaza Mayor.
T: (0034) 947 37 70 01
Beds: 30. Open all year. Has internet access.

Albergue Casa Nostra, Calle Real Oriente 54.
T: (0034) 947 37 74 93
Beds: 20. Open all year. Has cooking & laundry facilities as well as Internet access.

Albergue Camino de Santiago, at entrance to the town.
T: (0034) 947 37 72 55 / 658 96 67 43
Beds: 40. Open Mar - Nov.

Access to campsite restaurant, shops and bar

Camping Camino de Santiago, at entrance to the town.
T: (0034) 947 37 72 55 / 658 96 67 43
Open Mar - Nov. Facilities include restaurant, shops and bar.

Pension La Taberna,
Calle Rela Oriente 34.
T: (0034) 620 78 27 68

Hostal El Manzano *,
Avenida Virgen del Manzano.
T: (0034) 947 37 72 84

Hostal La Cachava **,
Calle Real 93.
T: (0034) 947 37 85 47

Hostal Méson Castrojeriz **,
Calle Cordón 1.
T: (0034) 947 37 74 00

Follow the main street out of Castrojeriz passing the Iglesia de San Juan and cross the road at a fountain onto a trasck on the other side.The track joins an old Roman road, which takes you over the Río Odrilla to the foot of Mostelares. You are now faced with the steep climb to Alto de Mostelares.

From the top you can see for miles back into Castrojeriz and onwards towards Puente de Itero, Itero de la Vega and Boadilla del Camino.

There is also a much welcome rest area at the top. Continue along the path which drops down past the Fuente del Piojo and a picnic / rest area onto a country road.

About 1.5km along the road, before crossing the river you can take a detour to the right and head into **Itero del Castillo**

Itero del Castillo

453km to Santiago |
Altitude: 780m

Accommodation

Albergue Municipal, in the Ayuntamiento, Town Hall, in Plaza Ayuntamiento.
T: (0034) 947 37 73 57
Beds: 12. Open all year.

Otherwise keep on the road until you reach the albergue at the 13th century **Ermita de San Nicolás**

The Ermita de San Nicolás is run by an Italian Confraternity and has 12 beds. Open Jun - Sept a shared candle lit dinner (there is no electricity) and breakfast is provided.

Cross the impressive 11 arch Romanesque **Puente de Itero** over the Río Piscuerga into the region of Palencia.

Follow the track right along the river past the 13th century **Ermita de la Piedad** which has a statue of Santiago Peregrino inside and a rest area outside.

Continue on into the village of **Itero de la Vega**

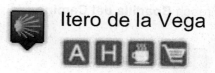

Itero de la Vega

454km to Santiago | Altitude: 770m

Accommodation

Albergue Municipal, Plaza Iglesia.
T: (0034) 979 15 18 26
Beds: 20. Open all year. Has laundry facilities and also offers Internet access.

Albergue La Posada, Calle Santa Ana.
T: (0034) 979 15 17 81
Beds: 18 in four rooms. Meals available in restaurant / bar

**Hostal Puente Fitero **, Calle Santa María.
T: (0034) 979 15 18 22

Head out of Itero del Castillo and climb the gentle incline to the top, which offers great views of the surrounding countryside. Continue downhill and alongside a river and carry on until you reach **Boadilla del Camino.**

 # Boadilla del Camino

446.5km to Santiago | Altitude: 780m

Information

The 16th century **Iglesia de Santa María** is home to an impressive 14th century stone font and nearby in the town square you'll find a 15th century mediaeval Rollo, stone cross, which is ornately decorated with scallop shells.

The Rollo marks the spot where criminals were once tried and if found guilty, executed.

Accommodation

Albergue Municipal, Calle Escuelas.
T: (0034) 979 81 07 76
Beds: 12. Open all year.

Albergue En El Camino, beside church and rollo.
T: (0034) 979 81 02 84
Beds: 50 in two dormitories. Has excellent facilities including dining & laundry and also offers Internet access.

Also offer private rooms in the adjoining Casa Rural.

Stage 15: Boadilla Del Camino - Carrion de los Condes

Map 3: Page 243 | Distance: 25km

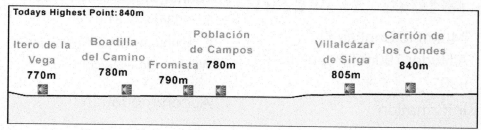

Todays Highest Point: 840m

Itero de la Vega 770m	Boadilla del Camino 780m	Fromista 790m	Población de Campos 780m	Villalcázar de Sirga 805m	Carrión de los Condes 840m

Boadilla Del Camino

446.5km to Santiago | Altitude: 780m

Continue through the village onto a track through barley fields and the Tierra Campo until you reach the **Canal de Castilla**.

The track runs alongside the canal, which was built in the 18th century to transport goods, especially crops and is now used for irrigation purposes. For more information about Cana de Castilla

Carry on for a few kilometres then cross over the canal at the Frómista Canal lock gates and head down a street, under a

railway line to a crossroads where you'll see the tourist office, turismo, only (open in the summer) in Paseo Central.

Cross over and head right then left into the **Plaza de San Martín** and the **Iglesia San Martín**.

Frómista

🇦 🇭 🍴 🍲 € ℹ️ 🛒 ➕

440km to Santiago |
Altitude: 790m | Population:
950

Information

Frómista, comes from the Latin
word for cereal, *frumentum*. The
surrounding area provided large
amounts of wheat during the
time of the Roman Empire

Frómista's most famous building
is the **Iglesia de San Martín**, an
11th century Romanesque
church built in 1035. It was once
a part of a Benedictine
monastery, which no longer
exists. The de-consecrated and
restored church, which is located
in the centre of Frómista, is now
the towns main tourist attraction.

Other cultural attractions include
the 15th century Gothic **Iglesia
de San Pedro** with its statue of
Santiago and a museum of

religious art. Also of interest may
be the stork's nest on the roof.

Tourist Office, Paseo Central.
T: (0034) 979 81 01 80
E: ayuntamiento@fromista.com
W: www.fromista.com

Accommodation

Albergue Municipal,
Plaza San Martin.
T: (0034) 686 57 97 02
Beds: 56 in six rooms. Open all
year.

Hostal San Martín *,
Plaza San Martin 7.
T: (0034) 979 81 00 00

Hostal Camino de Santiago **,
Calle Francesca 26.
T: (0034) 979 81 00 53

Hostal Sa Telmo **,
Calle Martín Veña 8.
T: (0034) 979 81 10 28
E: centroruralsantelmo@yahoo.es
W: www.turismofromista.com

Hotel Doña Mayor ***,
Calle Francesca 31.
T: (0034) 979 81 05 88
E:reservas@hoteldonamayor.com
W: www.hoteldonamayor.com

Head out of Fromista on a track that runs alongside the P-980 towards Carrión de Los Condes. On the outskirts of Población de Campos the track passes the 13th century **Ermita de San Miguel** on the left.

Turn right here down a small side street to the Paseo del Cementerio and on into **Población de Campos**

Población de Campos

434km to Santiago |
Altitude: 780m
Information
Población de Campos has a shop, restaurant and a couple of bars on the main street.

Accommodation
Albergue Municipal,
Paseo del Cementerio.
T: (0034) 979 81 02 71
Beds: 18. Open all year. Has cooking facilities.

Casa Rural Paso Camino Santiago, Calle Francescas.
T: (0034) 979 88 20 12

Continue along the Calle Francesca past the **Ermita de la Virgen de la Socorro** to a bridge over the Río Ucieza. From here you have a choice of routes to Villalcázar.

Alternative Route

Take a left over the bridge and follow the track that runs alongside the main road into **Revenga de Campos**

Revenga de Campos

434.5km to Santiago | Altitude: 790m

Information

Revenga de Campos is a small village, which is home to the Iglesia de San Lorenzo. You'll also find a small bar in the village.

Continue on straight into **Villarmentero de Campos**

Villarmentero de Campos

432km to Santiago | Altitude: 790m

Information

At the entrance into the village you'll come to a café and the Iglesia de San Martín de Tours on the other side of the road.

Again continue straight on through the village and keep going until you come to **Villalcazár de Sirga**

Villalcazár de Sirga

428km to Santiago | Altitude: 805m

Information

Here the alternative route meets up with the more pleasant recommended route.

Recommended route

Do not cross over the bridge and take the track that runs along the right of the Río Ucieza. Continue walking along the riverbank into **Villavieco**

Villavieco

444.5km to Santiago | Altitude: 790m

Villavieco's **Iglesia de Santa Maria** has a number of interesting Santiago related articles inside.

Leaving Villavieco cross the bridge over the river and turn right and walk along the banks of the Río Uzcieza. Carry on until you come to a small road at the Ermita de la Virgen del Río with its image of Santiago Peregrino.

Follow the road past the **Ermita de Cristo de la Salud** and continue into **Villalcázar de Sirga**

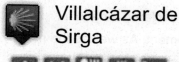

Villalcázar de Sirga

428km to Santiago | Altitude: 805m

Information

Villalcázar de Sirga owes part of its fame to the miracle cures, which are supposed to have taken place here in the middle ages under the statue of the Virgin Mary. Alfonso X mentions these miracles many times in his 13th century *Cántigas*, songs.

The monumental 13th-century Romanesque Gothic, described as the "Sistine Chapel of Romanesque style", is named after her.

Built by the Knights Templar the church is home to the tombs of nobles and royalty, including the polychrome stone tombs of the Infante Don Felipe and his wife Doña Leoner, and has recently been declared a national monument. As well as the many wonders inside, like the 13th century image of the **Virgen de las Cántigas**, and the magnificent 15th century **Spanish-Flemish reredos**, there is a remarkable double frieze on the main front.

The higher frieze features a central Panthocrator and the lower one depicts the Annunciation and the Epiphany, all-resting below a series of castled arches.

The church is open for visits: 10:30 - 14:00 and 16:30 - 19:00

Accommodation

Albergue Municipal Casa De Peregrinos,
Plaza de Peregrinos.
T: (0034) 979 88 80 41
Beds: 20 in 2 rooms. Open all year. Has a kitchen facility.

Casa Vidal *,
Calle Cantarranas 14.
T: (0034) 636 15 32 11

Casa Federico *,
Calle La Ronda 3.
T: (0034) 979 88 81 63

Casa Aurea *, Calle La Ronda 1.
T: (0034) 620 39 90 40

Hostal Casa Las Cantigas **,
Condes de Toreno 2.
T: (0034) 979 88 80 13

Head out of Villalcázar de Sirga on a gravel track that runs parallel to the road, all the way into **Carrión de los Condes**

Carrión de los Condes

🅰 🄷 ⛺ 🍴 ☕ € ℹ 🛒 ➕

421.5km to Santiago | Altitude: 840m | Population: 2,500

Information

Carrión de los Condes was a town of great importance at the time of the old pilgrimages to Santiago de Compostela and was once home to 14 pilgrim hospitals. Its medieval origins can be seen in its winding streets and in some of it's historic buildings and the old town.

The most characteristic building of Carrión de los Condes is the **Iglesia de Santiago**, famous for its splendid Panthocrator. It was recently restored after being almost totally destroyed during the War of Independence in 1809.

Also of interest is the frieze in the **Iglesia de Santa María del Camino**, embellished by an Adoración de los Magos and a depiction of the rescue of 100 virgins by a herd of bulls. The local Spanish Christians offered every year 100 virgins to the Moors. Santa María sent the herd of bulls and drove the Moors away.

There's also the **Monasterio de Santa Clara**, founded in the 13th century, with an adjoining church and museum, which displays sculpture and ornaments, as well as a Piedad, by Gregorio Fernández.

On the outskirts of the city, near the medieval bridge, is the 10th century Benedictine **Monasterio of San Zoilo**, a former pilgrims' shelter. Its outstanding 16th century Renaissance cloister is the work of Juan de Badajoz.

Tourist Office, Casa de Cultura. **T:** (0034) 979 88 09 32 / 979 88 03 94
E: fromista@caminodesantiago.org

Accommodation

Albergue Santa María,
Calle Clérigo Pastor.
T: (0034) 979 88 07 68
Beds: 60 in two rooms. Open all year. Has cooking facilities.

Albergue Monasterio de Santa Clara, at the entrance to the town.

T: (0034) 979 88 01 34
Beds: 30 beds in 5 rooms. Open all year. Has dining & laundry facilities.

Albergue Santiago,
Plaza de los Regentes 8.
T: (0034) 979 88 10 52
Beds: One dormitory.

Albergue Espiritu Santo,
Calle San Juan.
T: (0034) 979 88 10 52
Beds: 70. Open all year.

Camping El Edén,
Calle Tenerías 11 y 13.
T: (0034) 979 88 11 52

Río Carrión Youth Hostel,
Plaza Marcelino Champagnat 1.
T: (0034) 979 88 10 63 / 609 20 28 63
E: info@albergueriocarrion.com
W: www.albergueriocarrion.com

Hostal La Corte *,
Calle Santa María 34.
T: (0034) 979 88 01 38

Hospedería Albe *,
Esteban Collantes 21.
T: (0034) 979 88 09 13
E: hostalalbe@hotmail.com

Hotel Monasterio San Zoilo ***,
Obispo Souto.
T: (0034) 979 88 00 50
E: hotel@sanzoilo.com
W: www.sanzoilo.com

Stage 16: Carrión de los Condes - Terradillos de los Templarios
Map 4: Page 244 | Distance: 28.5km

Todays Highest Point: 885m

					Terradillos	
Villalcázar de Sirga 805m	Carrión de los Condes 840m		Calzadilla de la Cueza 870m	Lédigos 880m	de los Templarios 885m	San Nicolás del Real Camino 840m

Carrión de los Condes

A H A ▲ ♨ € i 🛒 ✚

421.5km to Santiago | Altitude: 840m | Population: 2,500

Head through Carrión de los Condes along the Cale Santa Maria into the Plaza del Generalísimo in front of the Iglesia de Santiago. Cross over the Río Carrión on the 16th century Bridge and continue on until you pass the Moasterio de San Zoilo on the left.

Keep straight on, crossing the new by-pass road onto a quieter country road, which takes you through farmland and across a few streams. After a few kilometres you come to the 12th century ruins of the Franciscan **Abadia de Santa Maria de Benivivere** on the right. The abbey was well known for its good living, benivivere.

The path heads straight to the Via **Aquitana**, also known as the **Calzada de los Peregrinos**, which the Romans once used to transport good to Bordeaux. The road runs straight across the plains passing the Fuente del Hospitalejo and crossing a few streams on the way.

The Calzadilla church tower shold come into view long before you reach the village. Continue on until you reach **Calzadilla de la Cueza**

Calzadilla de la Cueza

402.5km to Santiago | Altitude: 870m

Information

Calzadilla de la Cueza has a fountain at the entrance to the village and is home to the **Iglesia de San Martín**. The camino trail runs up the main street of the village.

Accommodation

Albergue Camino Real, at entrance to the village.
T: (0034) 979 88 31 63
Beds: 100. Open all year. Has laundry facilities and a small swimming pool.

Hostal Camino Real, further into the village. Has a restaurant and a bar.
T: (0034) 979 88 31 87

Head out of the village on the main street and across a bridge and the main road. Here you'll come to a map showing you some optional alternative routes that is if you don't plan on staying in Ledijos.

Alternative Route

One option is to keep on the main road; another is to take the track that runs parallel to the road past the **Monasterio de Santa Maria de las Tiendas** The path rises slightly before dropping across the road into

Ledijos.

Ledijos

396km to Santiago |
Altitude: 880m

You can see some images of Santiago in the Iglesia de Santiago. There is also a bar and shop in the village.

Accommodation

Albergue El Palomar.
T: (0034) 979 88 36 14
Beds: 52. Open all year. Has cooking & laundry facilities.

Head out of Ledijos and across the main road to meet up with the recommended route.

Recommended Route

Head left along track through a wooded area on the river bank, continue on this track until you reach **Terradillos de los Templarios**

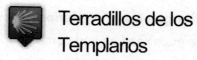

Terradillos de los Templarios

393km to Santiago |
Altitude: 885m

Information

Terradillos de los Templarios once belonged to the Order of the Knights Templar. The last Grand Master of the Order was Jacques de Molay who was burnt at the stake in 1314.

The villages **Iglesia de San Pedro** is built with red brick, as there was no local stone available. It houses an interesting 13th century crucifix.

Accommodation

Albergue Jacques de Molay, village centre.
T: (0034) 979 88 36 79
Beds: 35 in six rooms. Open all year. Offers cooking & laundry facilities as well as Internet access.

Albergue Los Templarios, on the main road as you come into the village.

T: (0034) 667 25 22 79

Beds: 56 over a number of rooms. Open all year. Has dining & laundry facilities as well as Internet access.

Stage 17: Terradillos de los Templarios - Calzadilla de los Hermanillos & El Burgo Ranero
Map 4: Page 244 | Distance: 26.5km

Todays Highest Point: 885m

		Terradillos de los Templarios 885m	San Nicolás del Real Camino 840m			Bercianos del Real Camino 855m	El Burgo Ranero 880m
Calzadilla de la Cueza 870m	Lédigos 880m			Sahagún 815m	Calzada del Coto 825m		

Terradillos de los Templarios

393km to Santiago |
Altitude: 885m

Take the road out of Terradillo de los Templarios and carry on across the arroyo Templarios and after a few kilometres you'll reach the small village of **Moratinos**

Moratinos

389km to Santiago |
Altitude: 855m

Information

Here you'll find a rest area and fountain beside the 16th century **Iglesia Parroquial Santo Tomás de Aquino**.

Continue on through the village on to the next village of **San Nicolás del Real Camino**

San Nicolás del Real Camino

386km to Santiago | Altitude: 840m

Information

San Nicolás del Real Camino is an old Knights Templar village where you'll find its ornate Baroque altar.

Accommodation

Albergue Laganares, Plaza Mayor.
T: (0034) 979 18 81 42
Beds: 20 in four rooms. Open Apr - Oct. Has Internet access.

Head out of the village and continue on until you come to a sign reading 'Senda de Peregrinos' that points to the right along the road. It's recommended that you go right onto a field path that runs along the river. The two routes meet at the 12th century Mudéjar style

Ermita de la Virgen del Puente next to a Roman bridge. Carry on towards Sahagún on the track along the main road. After passing the town's industrial estate you'll take a left after passing the white grain silos.

Continue on passing the town's bullring; take the crossing over the rail tracks into **Sahagún**

 Sahagún

379.5km to Santiago | Altitude: 815m | Population: 3,000

Information

It was here that San Facundo was martyred and a monastery, **Abadia de San Benito el Real de Sahagún**, was built in his name in the 9th century. The town of Sahagún came about as a result and is allegedly named after San Fagun, which is derived from San Facundo. The monastery became very important during the reign of Alfonso III de Asturias and more so during the reign of Alfonso VI de Castilla who bestowed many privileges to the monastery and town in return for the help he received from the monastery during his fight with his brother Sancho III. The town became very wealthy and the monastery very powerful as a result.

The monastery was very important on the pilgrimage route to Santiago de Compostela, and in the 14th century housed a University. In the 19th century, the Benedictine monastery was disbanded. Only the 12th century **Capilla de San Mancio**, the 17th century and the 19th century **Torre del Reloj** remains.

In the Plaza San Lorenzo you'll find the 13th century Romanesque Gothic **Iglesia de San Lorenzo** built in the Mudéjar style, as is the 12th century **Iglesia de San Tirso** in the Plaza de San Tirso.

Also worth a visit is the **Convento de Santa Clar**a also built in the Mudéjar style with it's adjoining museum which houses a statue of the **Nuestra Señora la Peregrina.**

Tourist Office,
Calle del Arco, 87.
T: (0034)987782117
E: otsahagun@hotmail.com

Accommodation

Albergue Municipal Cluny, 1st Floor of Iglesia de la Trinidad after the railway bridge.
T: (0034) 987 78 21 17

Beds: 85 in cubicles. Open all year. Has a kitchen facility.

Albergue Hospedería las Madres Benedictinas,
Convento de Santa Cruz.
Beds: 20 in five rooms. Open Apr - Oct. Has a kitchen facility.

Albergue Viatoris,
Calle Travesía del Arco 25.
T: (0034) 987 78 09 75
Beds: 60. Open all year. Has a
kitchen facility.

**Camping Municipal Pedro
Ponce**, Avda. Villa de Tineo.
T: (0034) 987 78 04 15
E: info@sahagun.org

Hostal El Ruedo *,
Plaza Mayor, 1.
Tel: (0034) 987 78 18 34 / 987
78 00 75
E: info@restauranteelruedo.com
W: www.restauranteelruedo.com

Hostal Pacho *,
Avenida Constitución, 86.
T: (0034) 987 78 07 75

Hotel La Cordoniz **,
Calle Arco.
T: (0034) 987 78 02 76
E: info@hostallacodorniz.com

Leave Sahagún through the old
town and past the museun and
the Arco de San Benito.

Cross the Río Cea via the
Puente Canto, which was
originally built by the Romans
and restored in the 11th century
by Alfonso VI.

The poplar grove next to the
Camping Pedro Ponce marks the
spot of the Legend of the
Flowering Lances when it is said
the lances of Charlemagne's
troops turned into saplings over
night.

After this event, Charlemagne
went on to lose over 40,000
troops in the battle against the
Moors. After a few more
kilometres the village of Calzada
del Coto comes into view. You'll
come to a junction and it is here
that the route splits.

Alternative Route

Keep straight on for the Real
Camino Francés, and follow the
path alongside the road, passing
the **Ermita de Nuestra Señora
de los Perales** before coming to
Bercianos del Real Camino

Bercianos del Real Camino

369km to Santiago |
Altitude: 855m

Accommodation

Albergue Parroquial,
Calle Santa Rita.
T: (0034) 987 78 40 08
Beds: 45. Open all year. Has cooking & dining facilities.

Hostal Rivero *,
Calle Mayor 12.
T: (0034) 987 74 42 87

Head through the village onto the path on the other side and continues along the road to **El Burgo Ranero**

El Burgo Ranero

366.5km to Santiago |
Altitude: 880m | Population: 3,000

Accommodation

Albergue Domenico Laffi, on the edge of town.
T: (0034) 987 33 00 23
Beds: 28 in four rooms. Open all year. Has a kitchen facility.

Albergue El Nogal, not far from the Albergue Domenico Laffi.
Beds: 30. Open all year.

Albergue La Laguna.
T: (0034) 987 33 00 94
Beds: 20. Open all year. Has a kitchen facility. Also has private hostal rooms available.

Hostal El Peregrino *.
T: (0034) 987 33 00 69

Recommended Route

The original path, Calzada de los Peregrinos offer a more pleasant walk. Cross the bridge and head into **Calzada del Coto**

Calzada del Coto

374.5km to Santiago | Altitude: 825m

Information

Here you'll find a fountain, shop, restaurant and bar.

Accommodation

Albergue Municipal San Roque, next to the pelota court. Tel: (0034) 987 78 12 33 Beds: 24 in two rooms. Open all year. Has Internet access. Continue on though the village on the main street past the **Iglesia de San Esteban.** Follow the track to the railway bridge, cross over and continue on the track passing nothing but a few sheep on the way into to **Calzadilla de los Hermanillos**

Calzadilla de los Hermanillos

366.5km to Santiago | Altitude: 885m | Population: 200

Information

Here you'll find the **Iglesia de San Bartholomé** with its statue of the saint fighting the devil. There's also a small shop and a couple of nice bars. The Comedor Via Trajana next to the albergue is highly recommended.

Accommodation

Albergue Municipal, at village entrance.
T: (0034) 987 33 00 23
Beds: 16 in 2 rooms. Open all year. Has cooking facilities.

Casa El Cura,
Calle La Carratera 13.
T: (0034) 987 33 75 02

Stage18: Calzadilla de los Hermanillos - Mansilla de las Mulas

Map 4: Page 244 | Distance: 24km

Todays Highest Point: 880m					
		Bercianos del Real Camino	El Burgo Ranero	Reliegos	Mansilla de las Mulas
Sahagún	Calzada del Coto				
815m	825m	855m	880m	835m	800m

Alternative Route

From El Burgo Ranero the route runs parallel to the main road. Cross the road on the other side of the village and carry straight on for roughly 10km until you come to a crossroads.

Cross over passing a few bodegas and carry on to **Reliegos**

Reliegos

349km to Santiago | Altitude: 835m

Accommodation

Albergue Municipal de las Matas, Calle Escuelas.
T: (0034) 987 31 41 03
Beds: 70. Open all year. Has cooking facilities.

Head out of the village and onto the path, which takes you straight to **Mansilla de las Mulas**. Enter the town through the medaeival Puerta Castillo in the Calle Santa María into the

Plaza del Pozo.

Recommended Route

From Calzadilla de los
Hermanillos, the route is really
just a striaght one all the way to
Mansilla de las Mulas along the
Calzada de los Peregrinos. Head
out of Calzadilla onto a meseta,
after a few kilmetres you'll cross
over the arroyo Solano, the path
heads towards a railway track.

Continue on to the bridge over
the arroyo Valle de Santa María.
The path now leads to a cross
roads where you have the option
of heading into Reliegos or
carrying straight on through the
Arco de Santa María and into
the walled centre of **Mansilla de
las Mulas**

 # Mansilla de las Mulas

342.5km to Santiago |
Altitude: 885m | Population:
1,800

Information

It is here in Mansilla de las Mula
that two camino routes join up,
the Camino Francés and the
Calzada de los Peregrinos.

The Romans built the wall
around the town as protection.
Since then the town has been
ruled the Gothics, the Moors and
then by the Spanish. Fernando
II, King of León, gave it town
status in the 12th century. At this
time the town was the largest
market town in the area.

The town name is taken from
Mano de Silla, '*hand on the
saddle*', which is also on the
town's coat of arms. The 'de las
mulas', '*of the mules*' was
derived from the town's livestock

markets. Mansilla de las Mulas was a very important pilgrim stop in old times and once boasted 3 pilgrim hospitals, 5 churches and many inns and hostels.

The 18th century **Iglesia de Santa María** with its Baroque altar and paintings is the towns oldest church. There is also the **Iglesia de San Martín** with some of its original Mudéjar style roof intact. The church has been converted into a civic center.

Also worth a visit is the only surviving town gate, **Arco de la Concepción**.

Tourist Information,
Calle los Mesones 16.
T: (0034) 987 31 01 38

Accommodation

Albergue Municipal,
Calle del Puente 5.
T: (0034) 987 31 01 38 / 987 31 03 68
Beds: 70. Open all year. Has cooking & laundry facilities.

Camping Elsa, by the Río Esla.
T: (0034) 987 31 00 89

Hostal La Delicias *,
Calle Los Mesones 22.
T: (0034) 987 31 00 75

Hostal San Martín *,
Avenida Picos de Europa 32.
T: (0034) 987 31 00 94

Hostal El Galle **,
Calle Cistierna 17.
T: (0034) 987 31 03 59

Hostal El Puente **,
Calle del Puente 11.
T: (0034) 987 31 07 62

Hostal Alberguería del Camino ***, Calle Concepción 12.
T: (0034) 987 31 11 93

Stage 19: Mansilla de las Mulas - León
Map 4: Page 244 | Distance: 17.5km

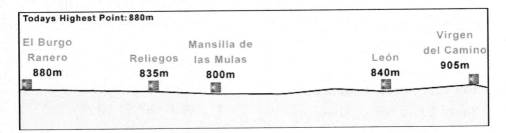

Todays Highest Point: 880m

| El Burgo Ranero 880m | Reliegos 835m | Mansilla de las Mulas 800m | León 840m | Virgen del Camino 905m |

 ## Mansilla de las Mulas

342.5km to Santiago | Altitude: 885m | Population: 1,800

Head out of Mansilla de las Mula, across a stone bridge over the Río Esla and onto the path parallel to the main road.

The hill on the right is the site of an ancient hill fortress and settlement of Lancia, Celtic Asturians, before the Romans in 25BC took them. Continue on for a few kilometres, crossing the Río Moro into **Villamoros de**

Mansilla with its **Iglesia de San Esteban.**

Pass through the village and after 2km cross the Río Porma via the Puente Ingente, a 20 arch bridge which leads you into **Puente Vilarente**.

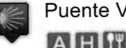 ## Puente Vilarente

336.5km to Santiago | Altitude: 800m

Information

There was once a donkey ambulance service in the village, which took sick pilgrims from the pilgrim hospice into León, but unfortunately this is no longer in operation. There are restaurants, cafes and shops in the village.

Accommodation

Albergue El Delfín Verde, Calle El Romero.
T: (0034) 987 31 20 65
Beds: 30 in different rooms. Open all year.

Albergue San Pelayo, Calle El Romero 9.
T: (0034) 987 31 26 77
Beds: 64. Open all Year. Has cooking & laundry facilities as well as Internet access.

Hostal Casablanca *, Carretera Adanero-Gijon.
T: (0034) 987 31 21 64

Hostal La Montaña **, Calle Camino de Santiago 17.
T: (0034) 987 31 21 61

Continue through Puente Vilarente and continue walking uphill, passing over the Canal del Porma and past a rest area to **Arcahueja**

Arcahueja

332.5km to Santiago | Altitude: 855m

Accommodation

Albergue La Torre.
T: (0034) 987 20 58 96.
Beds: 20 over 3 rooms. Open all Year. Has a kitchen facility. Also offer hostal rooms.

Take the first left if you want to detour to the village of Valdelafuente, or else continue on uphill past some factory buildings. Take a left when you reach the N601 road. If you want to stay at León's campsite stick to the N120 road.

Go as far as the roundabout, follow the path around it and

continue on the N601 until you come to a small foot bridge, you shoud be able to see León's cathedral from here.

Cross the footbridge and and head downhill until you reach **Puente Castro** and a tourist informaton at the bridge over the Río Torío. Puente Castro is now a suburb of León, which has plenty of bars and cafés.

Go down the Avenida Alcalde Miguel Castaño into Plaza de Santa Ana with it's fountain. Take a left at the **Iglesia de Santa Ana** into Calle Barahona and through the Puerte Moneda.

Just before you come to the **Iglesia de Nuestra Señora del**

Mercado take a right on Calle Escurial to the **Monasterio de las Benedictanas** and it's albergue in the old town of **León**.

 León

🅰 🅷 ⛺ 🍴 ☕ € ℹ️ 🛒 ➕

325km to Santiago | Altitude: 840m | Population: 132,000

Information

The Romans founded León in the 1st century and its name is derived from Legion. It became the capital of the old kingdoms of

Asturias and León and over time was conquered by the Visgoths, the Moors, and then by the Christians. It then became the centre of Christian Spain.

It sits along the banks of the Río Bernesga and is the last major city on the Camino de Santiago, before it climbs west into the sierras that separate Castilla from Galicia. León's cathedral, **The Pulchra Leonina**, described as the "Sistine Chapel" of Spanish Gothic & Romanesque architecture and the old Romanesque Hospital de San Marcos are the key points of this former Roman encampment.

The cathedral has undergone some restorations over the centuries in which a number of famous architects have participated. Ordoño II built the temple on the site of his royal palace to show his gratitude for defeating the Moors at the battle of San Esteban de Gormaz. His remains are buried here.

The stained glass in the Cathedral is from the 13th through to the 16th century. The three main rose windows, some thirty or more grand kaleidoscopic windows as wellas the many smaller ones cover an area of 1,765 square metres.

The Last Judgemet is dipicted on the cathedral tympanum. Adjoining the church is a cloister of which are many rooms, which contain a lot of religious art ranging from Romanesque to Baroque.

From here head northwest to the **Real Basicilica de San Isidoro** is one of the most notable and emblematic in all of Spain. It was constructed on top of an old church dedicated to St. John the Baptist and was demolished by Almanzor in 988.

Alfonso V rebuilt it and Fernando I reconstructed a new temple in which the relics of San Isidoro and San Vicente were placed, bestowing the church with an extra reverence. The style of the temple was Pre-Romanesque, and subsequently it was completely rebuilt in a Romanesque style, with three naves and a sanctuary with three apses.

One of the apses disappeared when it was converted into a Gothic style.

If you visit the church it is worth checking out the **Puerta del Perdón**, *Door of Pardon*. It was said that any sick pilgrims could pass through the doorway and be granted the same absolution as those pilgrims who made it all the way to Santiago.

The nearby **Casa Botines** was declared a Historic Monument in 1969. Antoni Gaudí started the project in 1891 when commissioned by the fabric merchants of León.

The result was a modernist Noe-Gothic building with a medaieval look. Today it is the social headquarters of Caja España.

Next as you enter the Calle del Generalísimo Franco is the **Palacio de los Guzmanes**. Construction work on this 16th-century building was never finished. It is the work of the architect Enrique Gil de Hontañón. On the lower part of the building you can find large openings with solid grilles and corbels with the arms of the Guzmans. On the upper part there are balconies with projecting sills and iron balustrades. It was declared a National Monument in 1963 and is currently the home of the Regional Government of León.

From here head west to the **Hospital de San Marco** was residence to the Knights of Santiago between the 12th and 15th century. The Romanesque facade was remodelled in the 16th century. The building is now one of the countries finest parador hotels.

The chapter house, *Sala Capitular,* houses a museum that includes weapons from León and Maragato artefacts from around Astorga.

You can pass through the museum into the hotel cloister, where you can see the magnificent artesonado ceiling.

Layout

The Train and bus station lie on the west of the cirty along the banks of the Río Barnesga. The centre of the city is on the east across the bridge near to the train station.

Cross the bridge and onto the Avenida de Ordoño II and make your way across the Plaza de Santo Domingo and after 1km you'll reach the cathedral.

From the cathedral there are plenty of bars and restaurants and you are a short walking distance to many pensiones and hotels.

Getting There & Back

Get a flight to/from León or Valladolid

Accommodation

Albergue Municipal, Calle Campos Góticos.
T: (0034) 987 08 18 32 / 987 08 18 33
Beds: 70. Open all year.
E: alberguedeleon@hotmail.com

Albergue Santa María de Carbajalas, Monasterio de las Benedictanas, Plaza Santa María del Camino.
T: (0034) 680 64 92 89
Beds: 180 in several dormitories. Open all year. Has a laundry facility. Also offers hostal rooms.

Youth Hostal Miguel de Unamuno, Calle San Pelayo 15.
T: (0034) 987 23 30 10
E: migueldeunamuno@terra.es

Camping Ciudad de León, 3km before León.

Hostal Reina *, Puerta de la Reina 2.
T: (0034) 987 20 52 12 / 987 20 52 00

Hostal Espana *, Carmen, 3.
T: (0034) 987 23 60 14

Hostal Orejas **,
Villafranca, 8-2.
T: (0034) 987 25 29 09
E: jamez@ono.com
W: www.hostal-orejas.com

Hostal Albany **,
La Paloma, 11 - 13.
T: (0034) 987 26 46 00
E: info@albanyleon.com

Hostal Casco Antiguo **,
Cardenal Landázuri 11.
T: (0034) 987 07 40 00

Parador de San Marcos *****.
Plaza de San Marcos 7.
T: (0034) 987 23 73 00
E: leon@parador.es
W: www.parador.es

Check:
http://tinyurl.com/hotels-leon

Where to Eat

Typical products, like the cured meats, cecina, which generally comes from cows and, sometimes, from young goats. This kind of meat is cured in the open air in the mountains and is the best-known product of the region.

The botillo, coming from the Bierzo region, is another type of typical meat of León and "chorizos" and potatoes and vegetables usually accompany it.

The Bierzo pie and Callos are usually found at the restaurants and taverns of the region. León offers a variety of vegetables, the

green beans and peppers stand out especially, wild trout, cured beef, thick pork sausage, spicy sausage, magnificent wines and traditional sweets are all available in León's restaurants.

The Maragato stew from the combination of some of these above ingredients is the most famous dish of León.

If you make your way towards León cathedral you'll see a lot of restaurants and bars in the area.

Local meal times are generally 14:00 - 15:00 for lunch and 21:00 - 22.30 for dinner

Tourist Information/ Oficina de Turismo

Tourist Information, Plaza de la Regla 3 (opposite the cathedral).
T: (0034) 987 23 70 82
E: monpriad@jcyl.es
W: www.leon.es

Open **Mon – Fri:** 10:00 - 14:00 & 17:00 - 20:00 **Sat:** 10:00 - 14:30 & 16:30 - 20:30 **Sun:** 11:00 - 14:00 & 16:30 - 20:30

Post Office / Oficina de Correos

Main Post Office, Avenida de la Independencia by the Plaza de San Francisco.

Open **Mon – Fri:** 10:00 - 14:00 & 16:00 - 23:00 **Sat:** 10:00am - 14:00 & 16:00 - 21:00

Medical & Emergency Services

Emergency Number for all services: 112

General Hoapital Yague
Avenida del Cid Campeador
T: (0034) 947 28 18 00

Comisaría: Calle de Villa de Benavente

Stage 20: León - Villar de Mazarife / Villadangos del Paramo

Map 4: Page 244 | Distance: 22km

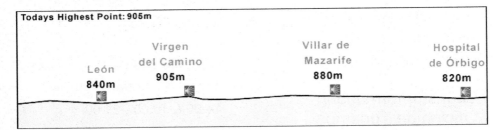

Todays Highest Point: 905m			
León 840m	Virgen del Camino 905m	Villar de Mazarife 880m	Hospital de Órbigo 820m

León

325km to Santiago | Altitude: 840m | Population: 132,000

From the cathedral, follow the scallop shales along the Calle San Pelayo and the Calle Fernando González Regueral to the Basilica de San Isidoro. Head past the church and down some step, carry on right along the town wall then turn left on to the Calle de Renueva.

You'll come to a crossing; on the other side is the Avenida de

Suero de Quiñones and the plaza in front of the Parador de León Hostal de San Marcos.

Cross over the Río Bernesga via the Avenida de Quevedo. Follow this road until you come to footbridge over the railway line into Avenida del Párroco Pablo Díez where the camino rejoins the main road at **Trabajo del Camino** passing the **Ermita de Santiago** with it's statue of Saint James.

Trabajo del Camino

324km to Santiago | Altitude: 840m

Accommodation

Hostal La Gárgola *,
Gran Capitán 7-9.
T: (0034) 987 80 61 80

Hostal Bella *,
Santiago Apóstol 8,
T: (0034) 987 80 28 10

Hostal Alfageme *,
Plaza la Huerta.
T: (0034) 987 84 04 90
E: hotelalfageme@hotmail.com

The route heads through the Plaza Sira San Pedro back to the main road passing some bodegas on the way. From here as you head uphill you get a good view of León behind. Proceed along the Calle Camino de la Cruz through an industrial estate and rejoin the main road into **La Virgen del Camino**

La Virgen del Camino

318km to Santiago | Altitude: 905m | Population: 3,200

Information

It is said that in the 16th century the Virgin appeared to a local shepherd, Alvar Simón, and invited him to throw a stone with his sling, making him promise that a sanctuary be built where the stone fell.

The current **Iglesia de la Virgen del Camino** was built on the site of the former one in 1961 and is managed by the Dominique Order. This sanctuary was built by the Dominique architect Fray

Francisco Coello from Portugal, and the sculptor José María Subirachs erected thirteen statues in a clear Modernist style. The 12 Apostles stand above the west door with Saint James looking towards Santiago.

The Baroque altarpiece of the temple with its depiction of the Virgin Mary is dated around the middle of the 16th Century.

Accommodation

Albergue Municipal, cross main road opposite the church.
T: (0034) 676 47 21 25
Beds: 40. Open Apr - Oct. Has cooking & laundry facilities as well as Internet access.

**Hostal San Froilán **, across main road opposite the church.
T: (0034) 987 30 20 19

**Hostal Central **,
Avenida Astorga 85.
T: (0034) 987 30 20 41

Hotel Villa Paloma *,
Avenida Astorga 47.
T: (0034) 987 30 09 90

After the church go left across the main road (N120) and then pass a small park and fountain. After about 100m you'll come to a fork in the road where the camino to Hospital de Órbigo splits.

Alternative Route

The Alternative route takes you along the road through Valverde de la Virgen into Villadangos del Páramo. At the sign post head straight on along the road onto a track that leads underneath a road bridge and then runs parallel with the main road into **Valverde de la Virgen** with it's

Iglesia de Santa Engracia

Valverde de la Virgen

314km to Santiago |
Altitude: 890m

Accommodation

Albergue Casa Floristeria,
Camino Jano 2.
T: (0034) 987 30 34 14 / 659 17 80 87
W: www.alberguefloristeria.com
Beds: 20. Open all year. Has cooking, dining & laundry facilities as well as Internet access.

Continue through Valverde de la Virgen and carry on alongside the main road into San Miguel del Camino.

Carry on the route alongside the road passing an industrial estateinto Villadangos del Páramo

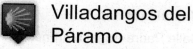

Villadangos del Páramo

304.5km to Santiago |
Altitude: 880m

Information

At the entrance of the **Iglesia de Santiago** you can admire two polychromed Baroque reliefs that represent the mythical victory of the Leonese King Ramiro I over Abderramán II in the fields of Clavijo, thanks to the help of Santiago Matamoros. The altarpiece in the centre of the church depicts Santiago Matamoros, with a sword and a three-cornered hat.

Accommodation

Albergue Municipal Camino de Santiago, entrance to the village.
T: (00334) 987 39 00 03 / 660 305 615
Beds: 80 in two rooms. Open all year. Has cooking & laundry facilities.

Hostal Libertad *,
Calle Padre Angel Martínes 25.
T: (0034) 987 39 01 23

Recomended Route

From the Virgen del Camino take a left at the split, away from the main road. Cross a bridge over a small road taking a right on the other side into **Fresno del Camino** and it's **Iglesia de San Andrés**.

Continue along a quiet country road down through a wooded area into **Oncina de la Valdoncina**, which has a fountain, and Iglesia de San Bartolomé

Take the track out of the village climbing slightly back out into the open countryside of the *meseta*. The track leads through the countryside until you reach **Chozas de Abajo** where you'll find a shop and bar in the Plaza San Martín. On the way out of Chozas de Abajo follow a quiet country road all the way into

Villar de Mazarife. Check out the medaeival style mosaic on the way into the village.

 Villar de Mazarife

303km to Santiago | Altitude: 880m

Information

The parish **Iglesia de Santiago** has several images of the Saint inside and many storks on the roof.

Opposite the church is the local bar. There's also a museum and an art gallery for you to wander around.

Accommodation

Albergue San Antonio de Pádua, Calle León 33.

T: (0034) 987 39 01 92
Beds: 40. Open all year. Has cooking, dining & laundry facilities as well as Internet access.

Albergue El Refugio de Jesús,
Calle Corujo 11.
T: (0034) 987 39 06 97
Beds: 30 in nine rooms. Open all
year. Has cooking facilities as
well as Internet access.

Albergue Tio Pepe,
Calle Teso de la Iglesia.
T: (0034) 987 39 05 17
Beds: 20. Open all year. Has
dining facilities as well as
Internet access.

Stage 21: Villar de Mazarife / Villadangos del Paramo - Astorga
Map 4: Page 244 | Distance: 32.5km

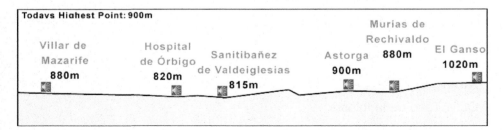

Alternative Route

 ### Villadangos del Paramo

304.5km to Santiago | Altitude: 880m

From Villadangos del Paramo head up through the old part of town onto a path that leads to the main road.

The path follows the road into **San Martin del Camino**

 ## San Martin del Camino

300.5km to Santiago | Altitude: 860m

Accommodation

Albergue Municipal, along the main León - Astorga road.
T: (0034) 987 37 70 86
Beds: 85. Open all year. Has cooking & laundry facilities.

Albergue Ana, along the main León - Astorga road.
T: (0034) 987 37 86 53
Beds: 48 in two dormitories. Open Apr - Oct. Has cooking & laundry facilities.

Albergue Vieira Carmina, along the main León - Astorga road.
T: (0034) 987 37 85 65
Beds: 60. Open Mar - Oct.

Continue through San Martin del Camino past the Canal del Párama turn right onto a tree lined path that runs alongside the main road.

When you arrive at the Canal Presa de Cerrajera the Puente de Órbigo comes into view. Follow the track until it meets up with the recommended route, which takes you across the **Puente de Órbigo** into **Hospital de Órbigo**

Recommended Route

Head through Villar de Mazarife across the road and onto a track which takes you out on to the meseta once again. Continue on to a cross roads and cross over and proceed straight onto a track which takes you across the Canal del Páramo and into **Villavante**

Villavante

293km to Santiago | Altitude: 830m

Information

Villavante is a small village with its 17th century **Iglesia de las Candelas.** There's also a bar and shop in the village.

Head out of the village across the bridge over the railway lines. Take a left and continue unto you cross a stream, Arroyo Huergas. Take a right at the road and cross over the N120.

The two routes met up at this point and head straight into **Puente de Orbigo**

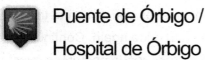

Puente de Órbigo / Hospital de Órbigo

289km to Santiago | Altitude: 820m

Information

Puente de Órbigo's name comes from one of the best-known stone bridges of the pilgrimage to Santiago. The 13th century 20 arch bridge is Roman in origin and undergone many restorations. There is a monolith in the middle of the bridge that reminds us of the love battle won in 1434 by the Leonese Knight and author Suero de Quiñones.

Suero gained fame by staging the Passo Honroso, at the Río Órbigo and describing it in his Libro del Passo Honroso.

From the 10th July to the 9th August in the Holy Year of 1434 at the Órbigo, Suero and ten of his companions encamped in a field beside the bridge and challenged each knight who wished to cross it to a joust. They swore to break 300 lances before moving on. Knights from all over Europe took up the challenge

He remained undefeated against sixty-eight knights in over seven hundred battles before he was forced to abandon his place after a month by the royal minister Álvaro de Luna.

Suero fasted in honour of the Virgin Mary every Tuesday, wore an iron necklet every Thursday as a sign of devotion to his lady, and heard Mass daily. The jousting tournament is created beside the bridge every year at

the beginning of June. On the other side of the bridge head into the village of **Hospital de Órbigo** with it's **Iglesia de San Juan Bautista** which was built around the pilgrim hospital in the 12th century by the Knights of the Order of Saint John.

Tourist information,
Casa Consistorial.
T: (0034) 987 56 86 19
E:
ayuntamiento@hospitaldeorbigo.com

Accommodation

Albergue Municipal El Camping, turn right at the end of the bridge and into woodland for about 500m.
T: (0034) 987 38 82 06
Beds: 28 in six rooms. Open all year. Has cooking facilities.

Albergue San Miguel,
Calle Álvarez Vega 35, opposite the parish hostel.
T: (0034) 609 42 09 31
Beds: 80. Open all year. Has cooking & laundry facilities.

Albergue Santa María,
Calle Álvarez Vega 32.
T: (0034) 987 38 84 44
Beds: 70 in three rooms. Open Mar - Oct. Has cooking facilities.

Camping turn right at the end of the bridge and into woodland for about 500m.
T: (0034) 987 36 10 18

Hostal El Caminero **,
Calle Sierra Pambley 56.
T: (0034) 987 38 90 20 / 619 87 00 69

Don Suero de Quiñones **,
Calle Álvarez Vega 1, right at the end of the bridge.
T: (0034) 987 38 82 38

Hostal Paso Honroso **, N120 km 335.
T: (0034) 987 36 10 10

Continue through Hospital de Órbigo on Calle Álvarez past the Iglesia de San Juan Bautista and the albergues. At the end of the village the route splits again.

Alternative Route

Keep straight on to the last buildings in Hospital de Órbigo and continue straight along the main road (N120). You'll reach the Crucero de Santo Toribio, on the outskirts of San Justo de la Vega where the track rejoins the recommended route.

Recommended Route

Take a right at the last building in Hospital de Órbigo and continue on the track into Villares de Órbigo with its **Iglesia de Santiago** and image of Santiago Matamoros.

Proceed through the village onto a wide dirt track across a stream into **Santibañez de Valdeiglesias**

 # Santibañez de Valdeiglesias

284km to Santiago | Altitude: 815m

Information

The **Iglesia de la Trinidad** has images of Santiago Matamoros and San Roque Peregrino

Accommodation

Albergue Municipal, close to the Centro Social.
T: (0034) 987 37 76 98
Beds: 60 in a few rooms. Open all year. Has dining facilities as well as Internet access.

At the church the path heads to the right and passes the albergue and some farms. The route now heads through some of the nicest countryside along the camino.

The track goes through oak woodland, orchards past a small lake then climbs slightly through open cornfields.

After passing some farms you will arrive at the **Cruceiro de Santo Toribio**, which was erected in commemoration of the 5th century Bishop Toribio of Astorga who, as legend has it, was banished from the town after being falsely accused. He stopped here to clean his shoes, proclaiming "I will not take even the dust of Astorga with me!"

It is here that the two routes meet. From this point you get a view of Astorga in the distance. From the cross the path now drops downhill into **San Justo de la Vega**

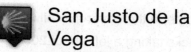

San Justo de la Vega

276.5km to Santiago | Altitude: 855m

Information

San Justo de la Vega is a growing town and has many shops, restaurants and bars.

Accommodation

Hostal Juli, Calle Real 2.
T: (0034) 987 61 76 32

Casa Rural Posada Viejo Molina Cela, Camino Molina de Cela.
T: (0034) 987 60 05 02 / 629 01 63 61
E: info@viejomolinocela.net

Leave San Justo de la Vega along the Calle de los Vientos and across the bridge over the Río Tuerto. Take a right and follow the track that winds it's way along the river valley. Cross the Roman Puente de la

Moldería then over the railway tracks taking a left about 200m later under the walls of the town and up through the Puerta del Sol into **Astorga.**

Continue through the streets Padres Redentoristas, Plaza de San Bartolomé, Pío Gullón, Postas, Santiago and Santa Marta into the **Plaza de la Catedral**.

 Astorga

271.5km to Santiago | Altitude: 900m | Population: 12,500

Information

Astorga was originally a Celtic settlement and later become one of the Roman strongholds in the region. Astorga is the capital of the county of Maragatos; a small ethnic and cultural community with distinctive customs and

architecture, in the province of León offers a rich medieval legacy, due its location at the crossroads of the Camino Frances and the Ruta de la Plata

The Roman city was founded in the year 14 BC and was then known as **Asturica Augusta**. It formed a strategic point for the transportation of precious metals on the Vía de la Plata. There are ruins of Roman baths that are still visible today.

The cities main monuments include it's **Catedral de Santa María de Astorga**, which was started in the 15th century and not finished until the 18th century, and displays a variety of architectural styles including it's Gothic apse and it's Baroque

style towers which depict a number of biblical scenes. The gilt altarpiece by Gaspar Becerra ia a master piece of the Spanish Renaissance with its Romanesque statue of the Virgen de la Majestad, whom the cathedral is dedicated to.

The cathedral's museum, **Museo de Catedral** has many fine exhibits, amongst these is a 15th century painting, El Puente de la Vida y la Reina Lupa depicting the burial of Saint James. Theres also the jewelled Reliquary of the True Cross and the 10th century carved casket of Alfonso III the Great.

Opposite the cathedral is the 19th century **Palacio Espiscopal**, which was designed by Antoni Gaudí for Bishop Jun Bautista Grau Vallespinós from Catalonia. The style of building and its excessive cost leds to a fall out and the building was necer consecrated as a bishop's palace. Today it is home to a museum of religious art called Museo de los Caminos, dedicated to the **Way of Santiago**.

If you visit the museum you will get the chance to view the palace's interior, which is decorated with Guadi's stained glass and tiles. On the Plaza Mayor you'll find the 17th century Ayuntamiento, Town Hall, with its Baroque facade. If you are nearby on the hour you'll witness mechanical figures of a man and woman dressed in Maragato style strike the bell.

Also worth a visit is the **Museo del Chocolate** on the Calle de Jose María Goy.

Layout

Astorga is easy to find your way around. The Catedral de Santa María de Astorga and the Palacio Espiscopal can be found in the north west of the old town. The Tourist office can be found on the Plaza Eduardo de Castro nearby and is open from Mon – Sat 10:00 to 14:00 and 16:00 – 18:00.

Accommodation

Albergue Municipal, Calle Matias Rodriguez 24.
T: (0034) 987 61 68 38
Beds: 36. Open all year. Has basic cooking facilities & laundry facilities.

Albergue Siervas de María, Plaza de San Francisco 3.
T: (0034) 987 61 60 34
Beds: 150. Open all year. Has cooking & laundry facilities as well as Internet access.

Albergue San Javier, Calle Portería 6, close to the Cathedral.
T: (0034) 987 61 85 32
Beds: 110 in four rooms. Open all year round. Has cooking facilities.

Hostal La Peseta *, Plaza de San Bartolomé.
T: (0034) 987 61 72 75

Hostal Casa Sacerdotal *, Hermanos La Salle, 6.
T: (0034) 987 61 56 00

Hostal La Peseta **, Plaza S. Bartolomé 3.
T: (0034) 987 61 72 75

Hostal Gallego **, Avda. Ponferrada 78. Tel: (0034) 987 61 54 50

Hotel Gaudí ***, Eduardo de Castro 6.
T: (0034) 987 61 56 54
E:reservas@hotelgaudiastorga.com
W: www.hotelgaudiastorga.com

Hotel Astur Plaza ***, Plaza de España 3 - 4.
T: (0034) 987 61 89 00
E: asturplaza@asturplaza.com
W: www.asturplaza.com

Where to Eat

Situated in the centre of La Maragatería, Astorga offers an excellent "cocido" which is served beginning with meat, then vegetables and finally soup.
As well as cold and salted meat, it also offers fine wines and delicious desserts. Don't forget to visit the Museo del Chocolate.

Local meal times are generally 2:00pm - 3:00pm for lunch and 9:00pm - 10.30 pm for dinner.

Tourist Information/ Oficina de Turismo

Tourist Office,
Plaza Eduardo de Castro 5.
T: (0034) 987 61 82 22
E: turismo@ayuntamientodeastorga.com
W: www.ayuntamientodeastorga.com
Open Mon - Sat 10:00 - 14:00 & 16:00 - 18:00; Sun 11:00am - 14:00

Post Office / Oficina de Correos

Main Post Office, Calle de la Brecha / Plaza de San Bartolomé.
Open Mon - Fri 10:00 - 14:00 & 16:00 - 20:00   Sat 10:00am - 14:00

Medical & Emergency Services

Emergency Number for all services: 112

Municipal Police:
Calle de la Brecha, 091

Stage 22: Astorga - Rabanal
Map 5: Page 245 | Distance: 24km

Todays Highest Point: 1480m

Murias de Rechivaldo

Astorga 900m 880m

El Ganso 1020m

Rabanal del Camino 1145m

Foncebadón 1425m

Manjarin 1440m

 ## Astorga

A H 🍴 ☕ € i 🛒 ➕

271.5km to Santiago | Altitude: 900m | Population: 12,500

Follow the camino through Astorga past the cathedral taking a left onto the Calle Portería and out through the Puerta Obispo.

Turn right into Calle Sancti Spiritu and continue straight on to the Calle San Pedro passing the **Iglesia de San Pedro** with it's mosaic of the Camino de Santiago.

Cross the N VI road at the crossroads onto a country road, Calle de los Mártires, in the direction of Santa Comba de

Somoza. The **Ermita del Ecce Homo** is on the left.

Continue on the path parallel to the road, which leads into **Murias de Rechivaldo**

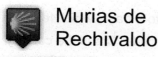

Murias de Rechivaldo

267km to Santiago |
Altitude: 880m

Information

The parish church, **Iglesia de San Esteban** was built during the 18th Century and holds an image of the pilgrim San Roque and has a carving of the Virgen del Pilar above the door.

There is a shop, restaurant and a few bars in the village.

Accommodation

Albergue Municipal, on the main road.
T: (0034) 987 69 11 50
Beds: 22. Open all year.

Albergue Las Aguedas, Last on the right leaving the town.
T: (0034) 987 61 67 65
Beds: 60 in three rooms. Open all year. Has cooking & laundry facilities.

From here you have two routes to choose from.

Alternative Route

Take the small country road beside the albergue and take a left onto the road that leads straight into **Castrillo de los Polvazares**

Castrillo de los Polvazares

265km to Santiago |
Altitude: 905m

Information

The village was originally in a different location but was totally destroyed by a flood, and rebuilt in the 16th century in its current location. It has been recently restored, and the buildings are typical stonewalled and slated roofed.

The main economic activity of its inhabitants is now based on tourism and handicrafts. Its main tourist attractions are its typical architecture and gastronomy.

Tourist Office Rural Casa Coscolo, El Rincoón 1.
T: (0034) 619 28 05 40

Accommodation

**Hostal Hostería Cuca La Vaina
****, Jardín.
T: (0034) 987 69 10 34 / 649 98 82 54
E: cuca.la.vaina@terra.es
W: www.cucalavaina.es

Hostal Casa Coscolo **.
T: (0034) 987 69 19 84

Walk through the village along the cobbled road turning left as you head out of Castrillo de Polvazares. Cross a stream and walk uphill where the path rejoins the recommended route from Murias de Rechivaldo.

Recommended Route

Continue past the pilgrim fountain and the albergue on the right onto a track, which leads to a crossroads. Cross the country road and onto the track that runs alongside the road into **Santa Catalina de Somoza**

 # Santa Catalina de Somoza

260km to Santiago | Altitude: 970m

Information

This area of the Camino de Santiago is next to the mountain Monte Irago.

The camino crosses Santa Catalina de Somoza through its main street, the Calle Mayor. Its parish church, **Iglesia de Santa María**, houses a relic from San Blas, the Patron Saint of the village.

The village had a pilgrim hospital before the 15th Century, known as **La Virgen de las Candelas**.

Accommodation

Albergue Municipal,
Calle La Escuela.
T: (0034) 987 69 18 19
Beds: 38. Open all year.

Albergue El Caminante,
Calle Real 2.
T: (0034) 987 69 10 98
Beds: 24. Open all year. Has a laundry facility as well as Internet access.

Albergue Hospedería San Blas, Calle Real 11.
T: (0034) 987 69 14 11
Beds: 24 in various rooms. Has café and bar facilities. Also offers private rooms.

Continue through Santa Catalina de Somoza along the Calle Real

back out onto the track that runs parallel with the country road (LE-142) into **El Ganso**

El Ganso

260km to Santiago |
Altitude: 970m

Information

As with many other regions of the camino, the festivities of El Ganso are dedicated to Santiago, and so is the parish church, **Iglesia de Santiago** with its statue of Santiago Peregrino. In the atrium of this church there is a small chapel known as **Capilla del Cristo de los Peregrinos**.

In the 12th century El Ganso was home to a pilgrim hospital and a Convent run by nuns from the Order of Cluny.

Some of the buildings in the village still have thatched roofs, '*casas teitadas*', in similar style to

an indigenous construction from
El Bierzo and Galicia.

Accommodation

Albergue Municipal, Calle Las
Eras.
T: (0034) 987 69 10 88
Beds: 16. Open all year.

Albergue Gabino, Calle Real.
T: (0034) 660 91 28 23
Beds: 30 in two rooms. Open all
year. Has cooking & laundry
facilities.

Continue through El Ganso onto
a track that winds it's way
alongside the road and
sometimes veers off onto forests
paths. On the right you can visit
one of the great Roman gold
mines, **La Fucarona**.

4km from El Ganso we cross the
Puente de Pañote over the
Arroyo de las Reguerinas. Climb
through mixed woodlands
passing El Roble del Peregrino
where pilgrims can sit on the
bench and rest in the shade. The

18th century **Ermita del Bendito
Cristo de la Vera Cruz** is on the
left as you enter **Rabanal del
Camino**

 Rabanal del
Camino

247.5km to Santiago |
Altitude: 1145m |
Population: 50

Information

The cobbled Calle Real takes
you through Rabanal del Camino
with its many churches and
hostels. It is a popular resting
point for pilgrims as it is the last
stopping point before tackling

Monte Irago and the Montes de
León. Inside the 18th century
Iglesia de San Jose there is an
image of Santiago Peregrino. We
can also visit the site of the
former **Hospital de San
Gregorio** and the **Casa de las
Cuatro Esquinas**, where King
Felipe II once stayed. The 12th

century **Iglesia de Santa María** with its ornate apse is worth a visit. During the 12th Century, there was a house attached to the church, which was occupied by the Orden de los Templarios, Order of the Knights Templar.

An order of German monks has taken up residence near the Plaza Jerónimo Morán Alonso and the church.

You can here Gregorian chant at evening Vespers at 19:00 and Compline at 21:30.

Tourist Office Rural la Posada de Gaspar, Calle Real 27 - 29.
T: (0034) 987 69 10 79
E: info@laposadadegaspar.com
W: www.laposadadegaspar.com

Accommodation

Albergue Municipal,
Plaza Jerónimo Morán Alonso.
T: (0034) 987 69 12 72 / 687 61 74 45
Beds: 45. Open May - Oct. Has kitchen facilities.

Albergue Gaucelmo,
Calle Calvario 4.
T: (0034) 987 69 19 01
Beds: 46 in two rooms. Open Apr - Oct. Has kitchen facilities.

Albergue Nuestra Señora del Pilar,
Plaza Jerónimo Morán Alonso.
T: (0034) 987 63 16 21 / 616 08 99 42
Beds: 72. Open all year. Has cooking, dining & laundry facilities.

Hostería el Refugio *,
T: (0034) 987 69 12 74

La Posada Gaspar **, towards the end of the village.
T: (0034) 987 69 10 79

Stage 23: Rabanal del Camino - Molinaseca
Map 5: Page 245 | Distance: 26.5km

Todays Highest Point: 1480m

Rabanal del Camino 1145m | Foncebadón 1425m | Manjarín 1440m | El Acebo 1140m | Riego de Ambros 920m | Molinaseca 600m | Ponferrada 540m

 ## Rabanal del Camino

247.5km to Santiago | Altitude: 1145m | Population: 50

From Rabanal the climb to Puerto de Foncebadón, Monte Irago, begins. The Camino follows a road along a rough track past the Fuente del Peregrino. Continue for 5km until you reach **Foncebadón.**

 ## Foncebadón

243km to Santiago | Altitude: 1425m

Information

Foncebadón is located on the top of Monte Irago close to the Cruz de Ferro.

In the 12th century Bishop Gaucelmo built a church and the pilgrim hostel of **San Salvador del Monte Irago** here.

Foncebadón was abandoned until the recent revival of the Camino de Santiago and over the last few years some of the buildings have been renovated.

It has two restaurants, a hostel and two albergues.

Accommodation

Albergue Domus Dei, adjoining the church in the centre of the village.
Beds: 28. Open Apr - Sep. Has dining facilities.

Albergue Monte Irago.
T: (0034) 695 45 29 50
Beds: 35. Open all year round. Has dining facilities as well as a shop.

Albergue Convento de Foncebadón.
T: (0034) 658 97 48 18
Beds: 21. Open Feb - Nov. Has dining facilities. Also has private rooms.

Continue through the village, and pass the ruins of the church and hospice built by Bishop Gaucelmo as you leave. The track rejoins the road, which leads up to the Puerto de Foncebadón and the **Cruz de Ferro**

 Cruz de Ferro

Information

Located at the top of Monte Irago, the Cruz de Ferro is a simple iron cross on top of a long oak pole, which stands on a large mound of stones.

It's origins remain a mystery, but could be related to an old pagan tradition where mounds called Montes de Mercurio, where built in honor of the god Mercury. This custom was Christianized after Bishop Gaucelmo is said to have placed the original cross here in the 11th century. The original cross can be seen in the Museo de los Caminos de Astorga. Adding a stone on top of the pile has become an important camino ritual with many pilgrims taking a stone from their homes to place here.

Beside the cross is the **Ermita de Santiago**, which although locked provides a nice resting place before continuing on your journey. From here a track runs parallel to the road down into **Manjarín**

Manjarín
A

238km to Santiago |
Altitude: 1440m

Information

Manjarín had a pilgrims hospital here in the 12th century with links to the Knights Templar, although its origins may be have been earlier and linked to Condé Gaton in the 9th century.

Like many other mountain villages, Manjarín was deserted in the middle of 12th century until 1993 when a man named Tomas Martinez renovated one of the old houses and started work as a "hospitalero".

Accommodation

Albergue Municipal.
Beds: 35 (mattresses). Open all year. Basic facilities. Outside toilet and water from a well.

From Manjarín continue alongside the road below a communication mast and a military station. Continue straight on past the turn off to the military station to the highest point of the Camino at 1515m / 4970ft. From here you start downhill into the El Bierzo valley. The Sierra de Gristredo and the Cordillera Cantábrica lie on the western horizon just above the town of Ponferrada. Continue on the downhill track into the village of **Acebo**

 # Acebo

230km to Santiago | Altitude: 1140m

Information

Acebo is a small mountain village, it's houses built with wooden balconies in traditional El Bierzo style.

The main street runs up the centre of the village to the **Iglesia de San Miguel** with its statue of Santiago Peregrino.

Accommodation

Albergue Parroquia San Miguel, beside the Iglesia de San Miguel.
Beds: 24. Open all year. Has cooking & dining facilities.

Albergue Mesón El Acebo, Calle Real.
T: (0034) 987 69 76 74
Beds: 24 in three rooms. Open all year. Has bar with pilgrim menu available.

Albergue Elisardo Panizo, first building on the right as you enter the village.
Beds: 10. Open Jun - Sep.

Casa Rural La Trucha.
T: (0034) 987 69 55 48

Casa Rural La Casa del Monte Irago.
T: (0034) 987 97 00 28 / 639 72 12 42

As you leave the village you

pass a sculpture of a bicycle outside the local cemetery. This monument was erected in memory of German cyclist Heinrich Krause who died here in 1987 on his way to Santiago de Compostela.

The paths leads along a country road then turn left onto a narrow path that leads into **Riego de Ambrós**

 # Riego de Ambrós

227km to Santiago | Altitude: 920m

Information

Riego de Ambrós is another small mountain village, and like it's neighours in El Acebo its houses are built with over hanging wooden balconies in traditional El Bierzo style.

The 16th century **Iglesia de Santa María Magdalena** has an interesting and ornate 18th century Baroque altarpiece.

Accommodation

Albergue Riego de Ambrós, close to the Iglesia de San Sebastián.
T: (0034) 987 69 51 90
Beds: 24 in rooms of four. Open all year. Has cooking facilities.

Pension Riego de Ambros *.
T: (0034) 987 69 51 88

Hostal Ruta de Santiago *.
T: (0034) 987 69 51 90

Head downhill out of Riego de Ambrós on a path that does get quite steep at parts onto a track that leads you past giant chestnut trees. Some of the forest has been destroyed in recent forest fires. Cross over a road and continue down the valley and back onto the road just before Molinaseca.

Pass the **Capilla de la Virgen de las Angustias** as you reach the town. You can catch a glimpse of the statue of the Virgin inside.

Cross the medaeival **Puente de Peregrinos** over the Río Meruelo into the old town of **Molinaseca**

  Molinaseca

221km to Santiago | Altitude: 600m

Information

Molinaseca is situated along the Río Maruelo. It's streets and grand houses display elaborate coats of arms signifying a once very important town.

It is said that the 11th century Queen of Castilla y León and Galicia, Doña Urraca once lived here in the house at the junction of Calle Torre.

It had up to four pilgrim hospitals and the 18th century **Santuario de Las Angustias**.

The **Puente de Peregrinos** over the Río Meruelo and the 17th century **Iglesia de San Nicolás**, which has an image if San Roque Peregrino, are worth a visit.

Tourist Office, Casa Consistorial.
T: (0034) 987 45 30 85
W: www.molinaseca.org

Accommodation

Albergue San Roque, on the main road.
T: (0034) 987 45 31 80
Beds: 30 beds and 50 mattresses. Open all year. Has cooking facilities.

Albergue Santa Marina.
T: (0034) 653 37 57 27
Beds: 56. Open all year. Has dining facilities.

Casa Rural El Reloj,
Travesía Fraga Iribarne.
T: (0034) 987 45 31 24

Hostal La Posada de Muriel,
Plaza del Cristo.
T: (0034) 987 45 32 01
E: info@lasposadas.com

Hostal San Nicholás **,
La Iglesia 43.
T: (0034) 929 79 30 53 / 617 79 30 53

Hostal El Palacio **,
Calle El Palacio, 16.
T: (0034) 987 45 30 94

Stage 24: Molinaseca - Villafranca del Bierzo
Map 5: Page 245 | Distance: 34km

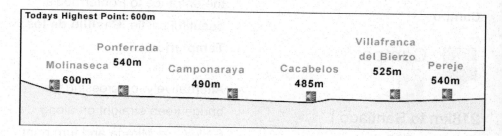

Todays Highest Point: 600m

		Ponferrada		Villafranca del Bierzo	
Molinaseca	540m			525m	Pereje
600m		Camponaraya	Cacabelos		540m
		490m	485m		

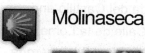

Molinaseca

221km to Santiago |
Altitude: 600m

Follow the camino through Molinesca uphill along the main road to the top of a gentle rise. Here you have a choice of routes

Alternative Route

Continue along the busy road into Ponferrada across a railway line, and heading left to an albergue.

Albergue San Nicolás de Flue, Calle de la Loma, off Avenida del Castillo.
Beds: 200 in rooms of 4. Open all year. Has cooking & laundry facilities.

Continue on the camino, turning left on Avenida del Castillo, then right at the Tourist Information onto Calle Peregrinos and Calle Temple and join up with the recommended route at **Castillo de los Templarios**.

Recommended Route

Turn left along a wide track into **Campo**

Campo

218km to Santiago |
Altitude: 565m

Information

Campo was once Ponferrada's Jewish Section. Some if the restored buildings have elaborate coats of arms displayed.

The villages **Fuente Romana** is still in operation and worth a visit if you have time as is the 18th century **Iglesia de Sam Blas.**

Follow the road through the suburbs of Ponferrada, passing the city dump into Los Barríos. Cross a stone bridge over the Río Boeza. Turn left to continue along the camino, under the railway bridge. Take a right onto Calle del Hospital then take a

left opposite the **Iglesia de San Andrés** and you will soon reach the entrance to Ponferrada's beautiful castle, **Castillo de los Templarios.**

Alternatively, on crossing the bridge keep straight on along Calle Cruz Mirada and turn right into Avenida del Castillo and then onto Calle de la Loma where you will find the albergue.

 Ponferrada

214km to Santiago |
Altitude: 540m | Population: 63,000

Information

Ponferrada, from the Latin Pons Ferrata, Iron Bridge, derived from the iron reinforcements added to the ancient bridge over the river Silis. It is the capital of the region of El Bierzo in the province of León, Castile y León, Spain. It lies on the Sil River, a tributary of the river Miño and has a population of 63,000. The region was an important mining area during the Roman period, when many different metals and minerals were extracted after the area had been conquered by the emperor Augustus in the twenty years BC.

There are numerous Roman mines in the area, one of the most spectacular being the gold mines of **Las Medulas** which were designation a UNESCO World Heritage Site in 1997.

During the second half of the 20th century the economy of the town was based on coal mining, but in the 1980s many mines were closed and the economy is now based mainly on tourism, agriculture (fruit and wine), wind power generation and slate mining.

The city is noted for the **Castillo de los Templarios**, a Knights Templar castle which covers approximately 16,000 square meters. In 1178, Fernando II of León donated the city to the Knights Templar to protect the pilgrims on the Way of St. James who passed through El Bierzo on their way to Santiago de Compostela.

The Castle hosted the Knights Templar's Grand Master of Castille. However, the Templars were only able to enjoy the use of their fortress for about twenty years before the order was disbanded and its properties confiscated in 1311. Several noble houses fought over the assets until Alfonso XI gave them to the Count of Lemos in 1340. Finally the Catholic Monarchs incorporated Ponferrada and its castle into the

Crown in 1486. As with many other historical sites in Europe, many of the blocks that at one point formed the walls of the castle were removed and used in local construction projects. Extensive restoration works are ongoing.

Since 1958, Nuestra Señora de la Encina has been the patorn saint of the Bierzo region. The 16th century **Basilica de Nuestra Señora de la Encina** with it's carved altar and statue of the Virgin Mary with child Jesus in named in honor of the patron saint.

The 16th century Town Hall, Ayuntamiento, and the 16th century Torre de Reloj leads from the Plaza de Ayuntamiento into the old town along Calle de Reloj. The 16th century old prison building on the Calle de Reloj is now home to the **Museo del Bierzo**.

Ponferrada hosts its annual festival, **Fiestas de La Encina**, during the first week of September with many concerts and activities for adults and especially children, and in July it organises a very popular **Templar Night** in its Templar Castle where participants dress up and recreate town life during the 14th century.

Layout
Ponferrada has undergone major modernisation in recent years. Anything worth visiting can be found in the old town in and around the castle.

Accommodation

Albergue San Nicolás de Flue,
Calle de la Loma off Avenida del
Castillo.
Beds: 200 in rooms of 4. Open

all year. Has cooking & laundry
facilities.

Hotel de los Templarios **,
Flórez Osorio 3.
T: (0034) 987 41 14 84
E: info@hotellostemplarios.info
W: www.hotellostemplarios.info

Pension Mining *,
Via Nueva 17.
T: (0034) 987 411 326

Pension Leonis Maciás *,
Almería 5.
T: (0034) 987 403 855

Pension King Jofra *,
Bishop Marcelo 10.
T: (0034) 987 401 478

Pension Triacastela *,
La Cierva 3.
T: (0034) 987 412 273

Pension Valcarce *,Trout, 9.
T: (0034) 987 411 137

Hostal Montecarlo *,
Antonio Cortes 24.
T: (0034) 987 455 703

Hostal Conde de Lemos *,
Avda Galicia 85.
T: (0034) 987 41 10 91

Hostal la Madrid *,
Antolin Lopez Pelaez 4.
T: (0034) 987 412 857

Hostal San Miguel *,
Luciana Fernandez 2.
T: (0034) 987 411 047

Hostal San Miguel II *,
Juan de Lama 18.
T: (0034) 987 426 700

Hostal Santa Cruz **,
Marcelo Macías 4.
T: (0034) 987 428 379

Where to Eat

In Ponferrada and its surrounding area you can enjoy a wide range of restaurants and mesons of various prices where you can taste typical products of Bierzo. The most popular of these as are the botillo, sausage, and variety of pies, Bierzo peppers, trout, and eel.

You can also sample delicious liqueurs like brandy, and local wines, some of which are internationally renowned as well as delicious desserts made from products of the region of Bierzo such as pippin apple pie.

Ponferrada is renowned for the production of six outstanding products of exceptional quality: Wine, The pippin apple, the pepper, the botillo, the jerky and the pear.

Tourist Information/ Oficina de Turismo

Tourist Office,
Calle Gil y Carrasco 4.
T: (0034) 987 42 42 36
E: turismo@ponferrada.org
W: www.ponferrada.org
Opening: Jul & Aug Mon–Sat 9am–12.30 & 2–7pm Sep–Jun Mon–Sat 9am–noon & 2–7pm;

Post Office / Oficina de Correos

Main Post Office,
Avenida General Vives 1.
T: (0034) 987 410 928
Opening: Mon - Fri 08:30 - 20:30
Saturday: 09:30 - 13:00

Medical & Emergency Services

Emergency Number for all services: 112

Local Police, Calle Ancha 46.
Tel: (0034) 987 446 627 / 28

Fire Brigade,
Calle de la Chopera.
T: (landline): 080

Hospital de El Bierzo
T: (0034) 987 455 200.

Health Center I (High Zone)
T: (0034) 987 400 611.

Health Center II (Polygon)
T: (0034) 987 410 250.

Health Center III (Temple)
T: (0034) 987 400 221 / 987 423 725.

Queen's Hospital
T: (0034) 987 410 059.

Clínica Ponferrada
T: (0034) 987 423 732.

Red Cross
T: (0034) 987 427 013.

From the albergue in Ponferrada take a left along the Avenida del Castillo, onto Calle Pregoneros and then Calle Temple towards the castle.

Before you reach the castle take a right onto the Calle del Reloj then turn left onto Calle Santa Beatriz de la Silva. When you reach Calle Calzada, continue down to the bridge leading over the Río Sil.

Alternative Route

Take a right at the Plaza San Pedro and then left onto Calle Río Urdiales followed by a right onto Avenida Huertas de Sacramento. Follow the road to Compostilla passing a sculpture of four women cooking.

Turn right at the Avenida Libertad and into **Compostilla.**

Recommended Route

Follow the route along a path beside the Río Sil. Cross the river and go down steps onto the other side. Walk underneath two bridges then take a left after a power plant and walk to the road where you rejoin the main camino route.

Pass a church with a statue of the Virgin and Child in front. Continue on past the **Iglesia de Santa María** and it's memorial to Santiago Peregrino.

The camino now heads through a tunnel under a ring road passing vineyards to the **Iglesia de Columbrianos.**

From here, cross the busy road into the village of **Columbrianos.** The 18th century **Ermita de San Blas y San Roque** is at the entrance to the village. Inside it has a beautiful carved Baroque altar and on the outside it has a small mural dedicated to Santiago Peregrino.

Continue through Columbrianos and onto a country road, which takes you through farmland into **Fuentes Nuevas.**

Fuentes Nuevas

206km to Santiago | Altitude: 505m

Fuentes Nuevas is a residential area and home to the **Ermita Campo Divino Cristo** with its pilgrim fountain. Opposite the chapel you'll find a nice café if you feel like resting for a while.

Proceed through the village on the main street and continue on for 2km to the village of **Camponaraya.**

Camponaraya

203km to Santiago | Altitude: 490m

In the past Camponarayawas a key point on the Camino de Santiago, as it had two pilgrim hospitals, the Hospital de la Soledad and the Hospital de San Juan de Jaberas.

Today it has a mixture of old and new buildings and the **Ermita Nuestra Señora de la Soledad.** Continue through Camponaraya and cross the Río Naraya to the other end of the village.

Go straight on past the Cooperativa Viñas del Bierzo and through a park with a fountain. The path now takes you through vineyards and woods into the Magaz valley crossing a stream and along a track into **Cacabelos.**

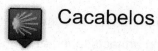

Cacabelos

A H 🍴 ☕ € 𝑖 🛒 ➕

196km to Santiago | Altitude: 485m | Population: 3,300

Information

Cacabelos was a popular point along the Camino de Santiago as it had five pilgrim hospitals.At the beginning of the 12th century the Archbishop of Santiago ordered people to settle here and build the **Iglesia de Santa María**, which was rebuilt in the 16th century and church tower added in the early 20th century.

On the bank of the Río Cua stands the 18th century **Sanctuario de la Quinta Angustia**, which is built on the site of a former pilgrim hospital. On the doors of the sacristy is the figure of the baby Jesus playing cards with San Antonío de Padua.

The village has a museum displaying artifacts found at the nearby Roman settlements as well as a wine museum celebrating the local wine industry and the history of its production the area.

Tourist Office,
Casa Consistorial.
T: (0034) 987 38 82 06
E: turismo@cacabelos.org
W: www.cacabelos.org

Accommodation

Albergue Municipal,
Plaza del Sanctuario.
T: (0034) 987 54 60 11 / 617 90 99 91

Beds: 70 in rooms of 2. Open Apr - Oct. Has cooking & laundry facilities.

Hotel Santa María **,
Santa María 20.
T: (0034) 987 54 95 88

La Gallega **, Santa María, 23.
T: (0034) 987 54 93 55

Hotel Moncloa de San Lázaro,
Plaza de San Lázaro 9.
T: (0034) 987 54 61 01
E: ponferradaplaza@domus-hoteles.es
W: www.moncloadesanlazaro.com

Continue along the busy main road (N-VI) passing through the small hamlet of Pierros and it's 11th century **Iglesia de San Martín**. From the top of the hill there are two routes into Villafranca del Bierzo

Alternative Route

Keep on straight along the main road passing the Arroyo Valtuilles and turn for Valtuille de Arriba. Stay on the main road until you get to a turn off onto a track, which takes you through vineyards where you rejoin the recommended route.

Recommended Route

Turn right then head left onto a gravel track through vineyards and into the hamlet of **Villatuile de Arriba**, which has two bars. Continue straight through Villatuile de Arriba and at the otherside cross a stream into Plaza del Fondo del Lugar leading onto a track.

Follow this track through hilly vineyards and beautiful landscape before descending in **Villafranca del Bierzo**

Villafranca del Bierzo

187km to Santiago | Altitude: 525m | Population: 3,700

Information

Villafranca del Bierzo is the last important town in Leon along the Camino de Santiago.

At one time there were eight monasteries and six pilgrim hospitals in Villafranca.

Its rich monumental heritage, and the influence of the St. James pilgrims, has made it an important tourist centre.

The Plaza Mayor, the Ayuntamiento, Calle del Agua, the arch at which it ends, the mansions, the **Convento del Agustinas Recoletas**, and other palaces, make up some of the more popular tourist attractions.

At the town's entrance we find the popular 12th-century Romanesque **Iglesia de Santiago**, a temple where pilgrims who fall sick and cannot continue receive the same absolution that they would in Santiago de Compostela, at the steps of the **Puerta del Perdón**,

Gates of Forgiveness. You should also take the time to visit the disproportionate 16th century Gothic **Colegiata de Santa María**, built by Gil de Hontañón.

Only the 13th century **Gothic Iglesia de San Francisco**, with it's beautiful Mudéjar style ceilings, remains of the former Franciscan monastery. The 17th century baroque **Convento de La Anunciada** is home to the Clarissa Order.

Tourist Information,
Avda. de los Escritores 6.
T: (0034) 987 40 61 71
W: www.villafrancadelbierzo.org

Accommodation

Albergue Municipal,
Calle Campo de la Gallina.
T: (0034) 987 54 26 80
Beds: 62. Open Apr - Nov. Has cooking & laundry facilities as well as Internet access.

Albergue Ave Fenix,
Calle Doctor Aren.
T: (0034) 987 54 02 29
Beds: 80. Open all year. Has cooking, dining & laundry facilities as well as internet access.

Albergue de la Piedra,
Calle Espiritu Santo.
T: (0034) 987 54 02 60 / 666 65 50 52

Beds: 38. Open Apr - Oct. Has cooking & laundry facilities.

Hostal El Cruce *,
San Salvador 37.
T: (0034) 987 54 24 69

Hotel San Francisco *,
Plaza Generalísimo 6.
T: (0034) 987 54 04 65
E: reservashotelsanfrancisco@gmail.com
W: www.hotelsanfrancisco.org

Hostal Mendez **,
Espíritu Santo 1.
T: (0034) 987 54 24 08

Hostal Burbia **,
Fuente Cubero, 13.
T: (0034) 987 54 26 67 / (0034) 600 64 39 64
E: reservas@hostalburbia.com

Parador de Villafranca de Bierzo ****,
Avenida Calvo Sotelo 28.
T: (0034) 987 54 01 75
W: www.parador.es

Villafranca del Bierzo

187km to Santiago | Altitude: 525m | Population: 3,700

Walk through the old town of Villafranca del Bierzo along the Calle del Agua. Turn left by the Plgrim Statue at the far end of Calle del Agua and cross the bridge over the Río Burbía.

A few metres later at the Calle Pradela, you have a choice of routes to Trabadelo.

Alternative Route

Continue along the main road (N-VI) until you reach the Puente del Río Burbia. Keep going straight untll you come to a hotel after a few hundred metres then take a right and continue along the road into **Pereje**

Pereje

182km to Santiago | Altitude: 540m

Accommodation

Albergue Municipal.
T: (0034) 987 54 26 70
Beds: 30 in two rooms. Open all year. Has cooking facilities.

Keep on the track along the main road into Trabadelo where you rejoin the recommended route.

Recommended Route

Take a right onto Calle Pradela up the steep hill onto a heather lined track that leads along vineyards. At the top of the incline you get great views of the surrounding countryside and Villafranca del Bierzo.

The path now leads you through a forest of giant chestnut trees at the highest point of the route at 900m. From here carry straight on along the track until you reach **Pradela**. There is a bar here if you feel like having a rest.

Continue straight on through Pradela and the chestnut woods on the otherside on a track that now winds steeply downhill into the village of **Trabadelo**

 Trabadelo

177km to Santiago | Altitude: 605m

Accommodation

Albergue Municipal,
Calle Camino de Santiago.
T: (0034) 987 56 64 47
Beds: 32. Open all year. Has cooking & laundry facilities.

Albergue Crispeta,
Calle Camino de Santiago.
T: (0034) 620 32 93 86
Beds: 20. Open all year. Has cooking & laundry facilities. Also has 7 private rooms available.

Casa Rural Ramón,
Camino de Santiago.
T: (0034) 649 82 74 97

Casa RuralPilar Frade *,
Calle Camino de Santiago.
T: (0034) 987 41 26 45 / 616 42
64 21
E: info@turismoruralpilar.com
W: www.turismoruralpilar.com

Hostal Nova Ruta **,
Carratera Madrid-Coruña.
T: (0034) 987 56 64 31

The path continues alongside the
main road. Pass the **Hostal
Valcarce **. T:** (0034) 987 54 31
80 and cross into **La Portela de
Valcarce**

 # La Portela de Valcarce

174.5km to Santiago |
Altitude: 610m

Accommodation

Albergue El Peregrino.
T: (0034) 987 54 31 97
Beds: 50. Open all year. Has
cooking & laundry facilities as
well as Internet access. Also has
private rooms.

Continue through La Portela da
Valcarce before turning off left
for Vega de Valcarce into
Ambasmestas.

 # Ambasmestas

173.5km to Santiago |
Altitude: 645m

Accommodation

Albergue das Animas,
Calle Campo Bajo.
T: (0034) 619 04 86 26
Beds: 20 and 10 mattresses.
Open May - Nov. Has cooking &
laundry facilities.

Residencial Los Sauces **.
T: (0034) 987 23 37 68

Leave Ambasmestas and after 500m pass the Albergue Do Brasil on the outskirts of Vega de Valcarce.

Albergue Do Brasil.
T: (0034) 987 54 30 45.
Beds: 36. Open all year. Has cooking & laundry facilities. Walk underneath a high road bridge into **Vega de Valcarce**

Vega de Valcarce

171.5km to Santiago | Altitude: 640m | Population: 850
Information

Vega de Valcarce with its **Iglesia de Santa María Magdalena** is a good place to rest or stay the night before making the steep ascent up to O'Cebreiro.

On the outskirts of the village on the hilltop you can see what remains of the 14th century **Castillo de Sarracín**. Opposite the Castillo de Sarracín is the remains of **Castillo Autares**, which was once linked to the Celts, Romans and the Muslims.

Accommodation

Albergue Municipal,
Calle Pandelo.
T: (0034) 987 54 32 48
Beds: 74. Open all year. Has cooking & laundry facilities.

Albergue Do Brasil.
T: (0034) 987 54 30 45.
Beds: 36. Open all year. Has cooking & laundry facilities.

Casa Rural Pandelo *,
La Calleja.
T: (0034) 636 18 08 62 / 987 54 30 33

Hostal Fernandez *,
Plaza Ayuntamiento 17
T: (0034) 987 54 30 27

Casa Rural El Recanto,
Calle Camino de Santiago 83
T: (0034) 987 54 32 0
E: elrecanto@hotmail.com
W: www.elrecanto.com

On the other side of the village continue along the road passing the **Iglesia de San Juan Baustista** before entering **Ruitelán**, which has a shop and a bar.

Ruitelán

169.5km to Santiago | Altitude: 670m

Accommodation

Albergue Pequeña Potala.
T: (0034) 987 56 13 22
Beds: 34 in three rooms. Open all year. Has dining & laundry facilities.
E: pequepotala@hotmail.com

Continue through the village passing the **Casa Rural El Paraíso del Bierzo** *.

T: (0034) 987 56 13 22.

Cross the 15th century Romanesque bridge over the Río Valcarce into **Las Herrerías**

 # Las Herrerías

168.5km to Santiago | Altitude: 675m | Population: 850

Information

Las Herrerías is named after its iron forge which it was once renowned for but has long since gone.

Today the small hamlet, which runs alongside the Río Pereje, has a number of shops, cafés and bars, one of which has its own restored forge.

Accommodation

Albergue Miriam, entrance to the village.
T: (0034) 654 35 39 40

Beds: 20. Open all year. Has dining facilties.

Continue along the road for a couple of kilometres then turn left onto a path that dips slightly before climbing steeply through a dense wood of chestnut trees. 2km later you will reach the village of **La Faba**

La Faba

165.5km to Santiago | Altitude: 910m

Information

With its 18th century **Iglesia de San Andrés**, La Faba is a small hamlet with a few shops and a bar.

Accommodation

Albergue Municipal, near the church.
Beds: 35. Open Apr - Oct. Has cooking & laundry facilities.

On the other side of La Faba the tree-lined track continues uphill to **Laguna de Castilla**

Laguna de Castilla

163km to Santiago | Altitude: 1150m

Accommodation

Albergue Privado.
T: (0034) 989 15 73 92 / 619 47 92 38
Beds: 15. Open Apr - Oct. Has a bar and café.

1km outside Laguna de Castilla you come to a stone marker announcing your arrive at the Galician border, Province of Lugo. Continue on the track for another 1km up into **O'Cebreiro**

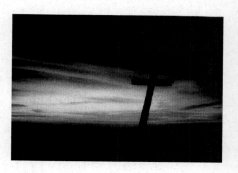

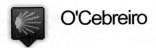 O'Cebreiro

160km to Santiago |
Altitude: 1290m |
Population: 50

Information

O'Cebreiro has a number of pallozas, distinctive round stone houses with conical thatched roofs, which were inhabited until relatively recently. One of them is part of one of the country holiday establishments in town.

The other is much older and has been converted into a small ethnographic museum, which is free to enter when open, usually in the morning and late afternoon.

A must see in O'Cebreiro is the 9th century pre-Romanesque **Iglesia de Santa María Real**, the oldest remaining fully intact church on the Camino Frances to Santiago de Compostela.

It is said that the Holy Grail was once hidden here in the Middle Ages. The churches bells rang during the winter to guide the pilgrims through the frequent mists.

In the 14th century a local farmer is said to have fought his way through a snowstorm to make mass in the church. The priest exclaimed his disbelief that the farmer would go to such lengths just to get a bit of bread and wine at which point the bread and wine turned into the flesh and blood of Christ. Both are on display in the **Capilla del Santo**

Milagro in silver phials donated by Queen Isabella in 1486 during her pilgrimage to Santiago de Compostela.

Outside the church you can see the bust of Don Elias Valiña Sampedro the parish priest who did so much in the 1960s and 70s to restore and revive the camino to it's former glory.

He travelled around Europe giving lectures on his work, The Way of Saint Jame, and in 1984 he marked the Camino Frances for the first time with the yellow arrows you follow today.

He was also responsible for the restoration of the Hostal San Giraldo de Aurillac, without a doubt the most frequented after Roncesvalles since it has been in operation since the 9th century. There are several shops, bars and restaurants in the area.

If it is a clear night it is worth a walk to the top of the hill behind the albergue for a wonderful view of the surrounding area and to catch the sunset.

Accommodation

Albergue, on way out of the village.
T: (0034) 660 39 68 09
Beds: 80. Open all year. Has cooking facilities.

Casa Rural Venta Celta *,
Parroquia O'Cebreiro.
T: (0034) 982 36 71 37

Casa Rural Frade *
Parroquia O Cebreiro.
T: (0034) 982 36 71 04

Casa Rural Carolo *,
Parroquia O'Cebreiro.
T: (0034) 982 36 71 68

Casa Rural Valiña *,
Parroquia'O Cebreiro.
T: (0034) 982 36 71 82 / 982 36 71 25

Hotel San Giraldo de Aurillac **, beside the church.
T: (0034) 982 36 71 25

Stage 26: O'Cebreiro - Triacastela

Map 5: Page 245 | Distance: 21.5km

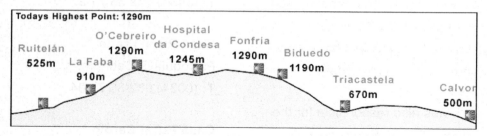

O'Cebreiro

160km to Santiago |
Altitude: 1290m |
Population: 50

From the Albergue you can follow the camino route for 3km into the village of Liñares or take the track past the albergue straight on past a rest area and into a small woods.

At the other side of the wood the path turns right and after 2km leads into **Liñares**

Liñares

157km to Santiago |
Altitude: 1200m
Information

Here you can visit the small 12th century **Iglesia de San Esteban**

Casa Rural Jaime *.
T: (0034) 982 36 71 66

Go past the church and climb uphill to the **Alto de San Roque** where a large bronze statue of a pilgrim faces Santiago and the oncoming winds.

The camino now runs alongside the road into **Hospital de la Condesa**

Hospital de la Condesa

154km to Santiago | Altitude: 1245m

Information

Hospital de la Condesa was once home to a pilgrim hospital from which it derived it's name. Today you will find the 12th century **Iglesia de Hospital,** which was partly restored in the 1960s.

Accommodation

Albergue Xunta.
T: (0034) 982 36 71 83
Beds: 18. Open all year. Has cooking & laundry facilities

Continue past the albergue onto the road, carry on until you reach a turn off signposted for Sarbugos. Take a right onto a

path that leads you through the hamlet of **Padornelo** with its **Ermita de San Oxan**. From here, it's a steep ascent to the **Alto do Poio**

Alto do Poio

151km to Santiago | Altitude: 1335m

Accommodation

Albergue del Puerto
T: (0034) 982 36 71 72
Beds: 50. Open all year. Local bar serves meals and breakfast.

Hostal Santa María do Poio **.
T: (0034) 982 36 71 67

Take the road right at the café onto the path that runs parallel to the road into **Fonfría**

Fonfría

147.5km to Santiago |
Altitude: 1290m

Accommodation

Albergue A Reboleira.
T: (0034) 982 18 12 71 / 61975
19 83
Beds: 40. Open Apr - Nov. Has
dining & laundry facilities as well
as Internet access.

Casa Rural Nuñez *.
T: (0034) 982 16 13 35

Casa Rural Galego *.
T: (0034) 982 16 14 61

Continue on the tree lined track
that runs parallel to the road then
turns right into **Biduedo**

Biduedo

145km to Santiago |
Altitude: 1290m

Accommodation

Casa Rural Quiroga *.
T: (0034) 982 18 72 99

Casa Rural Xato *.
T: (0034) 982 18 73 01

Meson Betularia *.
T: (0034) 982 36 71 72

From here the path descends
downhill all the way into
Triacastela through **Fillobal** and
As Pasantes where you can
stay at the**Casa Rural Caloto ***
T: (0034) 982 18 73 47

Carry on through **Ramill** and along the oak and chestnut tree lined track into **Triacastela**

 Triacastela

138.5km to Santiago | Altitude: 670m | Population: 50

Information

Tricastela gets its name from the three castles that once stood here, none of which exist today.

The **Iglesia de Santiago** has a carving on its 18th century tower, which depicts the three castles.

Stone was taken from a local quarry during the construction of the Cathedral in Santiago de Compostela. Medaeival pilgrims would carry as much stone as they could to the kilns in Castañeda over 100km away.

There is a pilgrim monument in the town built in dedication to those who carried stone to Castañeda.

Today you'll find many shops, bars and restaurants as well as plenty of accommodation to choose from.

Accommodation

Albergue Xunta, at the entrance to the town.
T: (0034) 982 54 80 87
Beds: 82 in fourteen rooms. Open all year. Has a laundry facility.

Albergue Xacbeo, next to Bar Xacbeo.
T: (0034) 982 54 80 37
Beds: 44. Open all year. Has cooking & laundry facilities.

Albergue Aitzenea,
Plaza Vista Alegre.
T: (0034) 982 54 80 76
Beds: 38 in three rooms. Open Apr - Oct. Has cooking & laundry facilities as well as Internet

access.

Albergue Del Oribio,
Avenida de Castilla.
T: (0034) 982 54 80 85
Beds: 27 in two rooms. Has
dining & laundry facilities as well
as Internet access.

Albergue Berce del Camino,
near Café O'Novo.
T: (0034) 982 54 81 27
Beds: 28 in 6 rooms. Open all
year. Has cooking & laundry
facilities as well as Internet
access.

Pension Vilasante *,
Camilo José Cela 7.
T: (0034) 982 54 81 16

Pension Aitzenea **,
Plaza Vista Alegre 1.
T: (0034) 982 54 80 76 / 944 60
22 36
E: aitzenea@arquired.es

Hostal Fernandez **,
La Iglesia 3.
T: (0034) 982 54 81 48

Stage 27: Triacastela - Sarria
Map 5: Page 245 | Distance: 18.5km

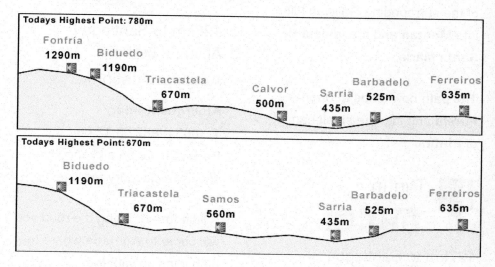

Triacastela

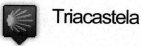

138.5km to Santiago | Altitude: 670m | Population: 50

Walk through Triacastela and on leaving the town you come to a junction. You have a choice of two routes to Sarria.

Alternative Route

This route is shorter and stays on the main road for less than 2km at which point take a left along the road into **Balsa**, passing the **Iglesia de Nuestra Señora de las Nieves**.

Continue on the path up through woods along the valley of the Río Valdeoscuro until you come back to the road where there is a fountain and large scallop shell.

Carry on along the road, which climbs steeply into **San Xil**. From here continue along the Alto do Riocabo, which offer great views of the surrounding Galician hills, into **Montán** and the **Iglesia de Santa María.**

The path now leads through **Furela** and into the small hamlet of **Pintín**

Pintín

127km to Santiago | Altitude: 630m

Accommodation

Casa Rurla Cines **.
T: (0034) 685 14 06 35

From Pintín proceed along the path into **Calvor**

Calvor

126km to Santiago | Altitude: 500m

Accommodation

Albergue Xunta.
T: (0034) 982 53 12 66
Beds: 22. Open all year. Has cooking & laundry facilties.

A little further along the road you will come to **Aguiada** where the path joins up with the recommended route.

Recommended Route

Turn left at other side of Triacastela and follow the road down along the Río Oribio and turn right to walk into the village of **San Cristovo do Real.**

Cross over the river and onto an oak and chestnut tree lined track which leads to a road at **Renche** where you'll find a bar if you feel like having a rest.

Head through Renche back onto the track, which leads through a tunnel before continuing down into **Samos**

Samos

120km to Santiago | Altitude: 435m | Population: 13,000

Information

The history of the Samos is closely linked to that of the monastery.

The Monasterio de Samos, built on the banks of the river Oribio, was the site of a community of hermits who gradually built the monastery in the 5th and 6th century.

The monastery, which has been Benedictine since the 10th century, is a combination of styles with its 12th century Romanesque doorway, 16th century Gothic cloister and

Baroque altar. During the war with Napoleon in the early 19th century, the monastery was used as a military hospital.

The monastery was almost burnt to the ground by fire at the beginning of the 20th century, fortunately it was rebuilt and visitors can still stroll through the cloisters, one of which is named after Padre Benito Feijóo and other is called Nereidas.

Padre Benito Feijóo, a native of Ourense who died in the 18th century and his memory forms part of the history of Galicia, lived and taught in Samos.

Accommodation

Albergue Monasterio de Samos, behind the monastery.
T: (0034) 982 54 60 46
Beds: 90. Open all year.

Albergue Casiña de Madera, on the outskirts of the town beside the 9th century Capilla del Salvador.

T: (0034) 653 82 45 46
Beds: 18. Open all year. Has
cooking & laundry facilities as
well as a massage service.

Casa Licerio *,
Calle Generalisimo 44
T: (0034) 982 54 60 12 / 982 54
61 62

Hostal Victoria *,
Rúa Salvador 4
T: (0034) 982 54 60 22

Hostal A Veiga *,
Compostela 61.
T: (0034) 982 54 60 52 / 982 54
60 42

Leave Samos along the main
road past a small chapel in
Teixos before passing through
Foxos and Teiguin.

It is possible to continue on
along the road into Sarria but for
the recommended route take a
right a couple of kilometres after
Samos.

Follow the path along the river

valley passing through small
hamlets and farms before
crossing a small stream and up
to Aguiada where the two paths
join.

Take the track along the road
through San Mamed del
Camino

 San Mamed del
Camino

Accommodation

Albergue Paloma y Leña, just
off the road.
T: (0034) 658 90 68 16
Beds: 30 in two rooms. Open all
year. Has dining facilities. Also
offers private rooms.

Proceed along the track passing
the campsite, which rents tents
and has bar & restaurant
facilities.
T: (0034) 982 53 54 67

Continue on until you reach Vigo
de Sarria

Vigo de Sarria

Accommodation

Albergue A Pedra.
T: (0034) 982 53 01 30
Beds: 15. Open all year. Has cooking & laundry facilities.

Carry on past the tourist office until you reach the Puente Ribeira over the Río Sarria. Turn right on the other side of the bridge and climb the **Escalinata Maior**, granite steps, into the Rúa Maior

Sarria

A H ⛺ 🍴 🍽 € ℹ 🛒 ➕

120km to Santiago | Altitude: 435m | Population: 13,000

Information

The last king of León, King Alfonso IX, founded Sarria in the 13th century. He died here in 1230 whilst on a pilgrimage to Santiago.

The town went on to be one of the major points along the Camino de Santiago boasting several churches, monasteries and chapels as well as seven pilgrim hospitals.

At the entrance of the town is the 13th century **Convento de la Magdalena,** which was founded as a hostel by two Italian pilgrims and is now home to the Order of Mercedarians.

The 13th century Gothic **Iglesia de San Salvador** with it's ornate door stands next to the County Court building, which until the mid 19th century was a pilgrim hospital.

The Rúa Maior, which runs through the centre of the old town, is lined with grand 18th century houses and leads all the way up to the site of the ruined castle, Fortaleza de Sarria. Only the fortress tower is still preserved. A cattle and food market is help here on the 6th, 20th and 27th of the month.

Accommodation

Albergue Xunta,
Calle Mayor 79.
T: (0034) 660 39 68 13
Beds: 40. Open all year. Has cooking & laundry facilities.

Albergue Don Álvaro,
Rúa Maior 10
T: (0034) 982 53 15 92
Beds: 40. Open all year. Has cooking & laundry facilities as well as Internet access.

Albergue Los Blasones,
Rúa Maior 31
T: (0034) 600 51 25 65
Beds: 30. Open all year. Has cooking & laundry facilities.

Albergue O Durmiñento,
Rúa Maior 44
T: (0034) 982 53 10 99
Beds: 42. Open all year. Has cooking & laundry facilities

as well as Internet access.

Albergue Internacional,
Rúa Maior 57
T: (0034) 982 53 51 09
Beds: 58. Open all year. Has cooking, dining & laundry facilities as well as Internet access.

Albergue Dos Oito Marabedís,
Rúa Conde de Lemos 23
T: (0034) 629 46 17 70
Beds: 19. Open all year. Has cooking & laundry facilities as well as Internet access.

Hotel Roma **,
Calle Calvo Sotelo 2
T: (0034) 982 53 22 11 / 982 53 05 70

Hotel Oca Villa de Sarria **,
Calle Benigno Quiroga 49.
T: (0034) 982 53 38 73

Hotel Alfonso XI ***,
Rúa do Peregrino 29
T: (0034) 982 53 00 05

Stage 28: Sarria - Portomarín
Map 6: Page 246 | Distance: 22.5km

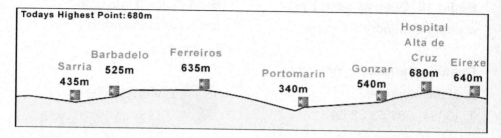

 ## Sarria

🅰️ 🅷️ ⛺ 🍴 ☕ €️ ℹ️ 🛒 ➕

120km to Santiago |
Altitude: 435m | Population:
13,000

Walk along the Rúa Maior and
take a left just as you come to
the **Convento de la Magdalena.**

Pass the ruins of the Capela de

San Lázaru then cross the road
and over the Río Celeiro via the
Puente Áspera.

Follow the track along the
railway line and then cross over
the track, then a stream and
begin the climb up through
woodland. Rejoin the road at
Vilei, which leads into
Barbadello

Barbadello

🅰️ 🅷️ 🍴 ☕

116km to Santiago |
Altitude: 525m
Accommodation

Albergue Municipal.

T: (0034) 982 53 04 12 / 686 74
40 48
Beds: 18. Open all year. Has
cooking & laundry facilities.

Casa de Carmen, 200m uphill
past the albergue.
T: (0034) 982 53 22 94
Beds: 10. Open all year. Has
dining facilities. Also has private
rooms.

From Barbadelos continue along
the road through woodland into
Rente, which has a couple of
bars and a shop

 # Rente

115km to Santiago |
Altitude: 595m

Accommodation

Casa Nova de Rente *.
T: (0034) 982 18 78 54

Go through Rente and in less
then a kilometre you will reach
Peruscallo which has a bar and
restaurant.

The camino passes through the
small hamlets of **Cortiñas** and
Brea passing the 100km to
Santiago stone marker into
Morgade.

 # Morgade

109km to Santiago |
Altitude: 655m

Accommodation

Casa Morgade with adjoining
café and bar. Tel: (0034) 982 53
12 50.

On the other side of the village
we pass a small stone chapel
and follow the country lane on
the gentle ascent into **Ferreiros**
which has a bar and restaurant.

 # Ferreiros

107.5km to Santiago |
Altitude: 635m

Accommodation

Albergue Municipal.
T: (0034) 686 74 49 40.
Beds: 22. Open all year. Has cooking facilities.

Continue to **Mirallos, which** has a café/restaurant beside the **Iglesia de Santa María**.

Continue along the road through the hamlets of **Pena**, **Couto** and **Rozas** before arriving in **Mercadoiro**

Mercadoiro

103.5km to Santiago | Altitude: 490m

Accommodation

Albergue La Bodeguiña. Tel: (0034) 676 47 62 60
Beds: 25. Open all year. Has cooking & laundry facilities. Also has an adjoining café/restaurant.

Proceed through Mercadero along the road passing more small hamlets along the way, including **Parrocha**, until you

arrive at **Vilachá**

Continue on the road and then cross the bridge over the Río Miño.

On the other side of the bridge climb the steps that were once part of the original mediaeval bridge that crossed the river.

The steps take you up through an arch to the **Iglesia de Santa María de la Nieves**, which was moved here in 1962 to make way for the dam.

Take a left if you want to continue on the camino or take a right, past a park and fountain up into the old town of **Portomarín**.

Portomarín

A H 🍴 ☕ € 🛒 ➕

97.5km to Santiago | Altitude: 340m | Population: 2,000

Information

In the 1960s the Río Miño was dammed to create the Belesar reservoir. The old village of Portomarín is now under water. The most historic monuments where moved brick by brick up into the new town.

The 12th century Romanesque **Iglesia de San Nicola**s looks more like a castle than a church and is the work of a student of Mateo, who was the creator of the Pórtico de la Gloria in Santiago Cathedral.

It is sometimes called the **Iglesia de San Juan** or **San Xoán** because of it's close connections with the Order of the Knights of Saint John.

If you take a look at the external brickwork you can still see numbers on each brick from the time it was moved.

Accommodation

Albergue Municipal,
Carretera de Lugo.
T: (0034) 982 54 51 43
Beds: 100. Open all year. Has cooking & laundry facilities.

Albergue Ferramenteiro,
Calle Chantada.
T: (0034) 982 54 53 62
Beds: 120. Open all year. Has cooking & laundry facilities as

well as Internet access.

Albergue Mirador,
Calle Chantada.
T: (0034) 982 54 53 23
Beds: 27. Open all year. Has
dining & laundry facilities as well
as Internet access.

Albergue El Caminante,
Calle Rúa Sánchez Carro.
T: (0034) 982 54 51 76
Beds: 48. Open Apr - Oct. Has
laundry facilities.

Hotel Villajardín **,
Rúa do Miño 14.
T: (0034) 982 54 52 52

Pensión Arenas **,
Plaza Condes Fenosa.
T: (0034) 982 54 53 86

Hostal Posada de Portomarín
**, Avenida de Sarria.
T: (0034) 982 54 52 00

Stage 29: Portomarín - Palas de Rei
Map 6: Page 246 | Distance: 24.5km

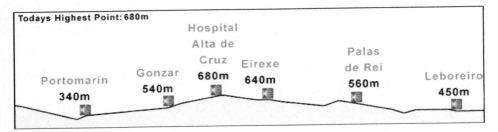

Todays Highest Point: 680m

		Hospital Alta de Cruz			Palas de Rei		
Portomarín 340m	Gonzar 540m	680m	Eirexe 640m		560m	Leboreiro 450m	

Portomarín

97.5km to Santiago | Altitude: 340m | Population: 2,000

Walk down the main street of Portomarín past the **Escalinata de Nuestra Señora de las Nieves**, Stairs of Our Lady of the Snow. Take a right and cross over a metal footbridge over the Río Torres.

Turn right on the other side of the bridge and head uphill through an oak forest. Cross the road at the ceramic factory and back onto the path that takes you through **Toxibó**. The path continues to run parallel to the road into **Gonzar**.

Gonzar

89.5km to Santiago | Altitude: 540m

Accommodation

Albergue Municipal, on the main road.
T: (0034) 982 15 78 40

Beds: 20. Open all year. Has cooking & laundry facilities.

Albergue Casa Garcia.
T: (0034) 982 15 78 42
Beds: 26. Open all year. Has dining & laundry facilities. Also offers private rooms.

Head out of the village along the road past a bar/café and turn right onto a small track. After 1km or so you will arrive at **Castromaior**

Castromaior

88.5km to Santiago | Altitude: 600m

Information

Named after a Celtic Castro that once stood here, Castromaior, is a small village with its **Iglesia de Santa María** and a small café

Accommodation

Pension Casa Maruja *
T: (0034) 982 18 90 54

Continue through the village onto the path to **Hospital de la Cruz**

Hospital de la Cruz

86.5km to Santiago | Altitude: 680m

Accommodation

Albergue Municipal
T: (0034) 982 54 52 32
Beds: 22 in two rooms. Open all year. Has cooking & laundry facilities.

Proceed along the country road into **Ventas de Narón**

Ventas de Narón

85.5km to Santiago |
Altitude: 700m

Information

The surrounding area is the site
of a 9th century battle between
the northern Christian kingdoms
and the Arabs.

Today you'll find the small
**Ermita de Santa María
Magdalene** and a couple of
cafés.

Accommodation

Albergue Casa Molar.
T: (0034) 696 79 45 07
Beds: 22. Open all year. Has
dining facilities. Also has private
rooms.

Albergue O Cruceiro.
T: (0034) 658 06 49 17
Beds: 25. Open all year. Has
dining facilities. Also has private
rooms.

Climb out of the village over the
Sierra Ligonde, the high point of
todays walk at 725m. Walk down

through **Previsa** and **Lameiros**
where you'll find a beautiful 17th
century stone cruceiro on the left
before entering **Ligonde**

Ligonde

82km to Santiago | Altitude:
630m

Information

Ligonde was once a popular
resting point along the camino
and had a pilgrim hospital. The
Iglesia de Santiago has a nice
Romanesque doorway.

Accommodation

**Albergue Municipal Escuela de
Ligonde**.
Beds: 22. Open all year. Has
cooking & laundry facilties.

**Albergue Fuente del
Peregrino**.
T: (0034) 982 18 37 52
Beds: 10. Jun - Aug. Has dining
facilties.1km further along the
path is **Eirexe**

Eirexe

80.5km to Santiago |
Altitude: 640m

Accommodation

Albergue Municipal, at village junction.
T: (0034) 982 15 34 83
Beds: 18. Open all year. Has cooking & laundry facilties.

Pensión Cantina *.
T: (0034) 982 37 74 61

Pensión Eirexe *.
T: (0034) 982 15 34 75

Continue along the path through the hamlet of **Porto** and then into **A Calzada**

A Calzada

Accommodation

Albergue Calzada. Tel: (0034) 982 18 37 44
Beds: 10.Open all year. Has dining facilties.

From here there is a possible detour on the right (2km) to see the 14th century **Monasterio de San Salvador** at **Vilar de Donas.**

It is a national monument and is the burial place of the Knights of Santiago. Continue along the path through the hamlets of **Lestedo**, **Valos**, **Mamurria** and **Brea**.

From Brea keep on the track that runs next to a rest area and climb up to **Alto Rosario**.

 # Alto Rosario

74.5km to Santiago | Altitude: 610m

Information

If it's a good day you should be able to see the Monte Pico Sacro, which is just above Santiago de Compostela.

Accommodation

Albergue Os Chacotes.
Beds: 112 in two rooms. Open all year. Has cooking & laundry facilties.

The camino now goes past the **Hotel La Cabana *****
T: (0034) 982 38 07 50, and a sports stadium before heading down into **Palas de Re**

 # Palas de Rei

73km to Santiago | Altitude: 560m | Population: 4,200

Information

Once home to a King's palace, there is little left to remind you of Palas de Rei's colourful past. The **Iglesia de San Tirso** has a nice Romanesque doorway and scallop shell motifs.

The visual high point of Palas de Rei would have to be the Plaza Concello from which much of the rest of the town radiates. There is also the typical Galician Ayuntamiento, Town Hall, built with a mixture of granite and whitewashed render.

You will see similar civic buildings in nearly every town in the region. Palas de Rey also has a number of shops, bars and cafes.

Accommodation

Albergue Municipal,
Plaza Concello.
T: (0034) 982 37 41 26
Beds: 60 in six rooms. Open all year. Has cooking facilities.

Albergue Buen Camino,
Rúa del Peregrino.
T: (0034) 982 38 02 33
Beds: 41 in six rooms. Open all year. Has cooking & laundry facilities as well as Internet access.

Pensión Guntina *,
Travesia do Peregrino 4.
T: (0034) 982 38 00 80

Hotel Vilariño **,
Avenida de Compostela 16.
T: (0034) 982 38 01 52

Hotel Benilde **, Calle del Mercado. Tel (0034) 982 38 07 17

Stage 30: Palas de Rei - Ribadiso do Baixo
Map 6: Page 246 | Distance: 27km

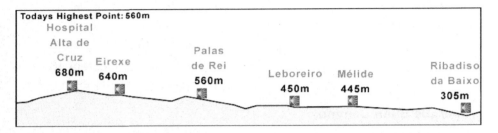

Palas de Rei

73km to Santiago | Altitude: 560m | Population: 4,200

From the other side of Palas de Rei walk along the road to **Carballal**.

Cross over the road onto a path through woodland before arriving

at **San Xulián do Camino** with its 12th century **Iglesia de San Xulián**

San Xulián do Camino

69km to Santiago | Altitude: 480m

Accommodation

Albergue O Abrigadoiro.
T: (0034) 676 59 69 75
Beds: 16. Open all year. Has dining facilities.

The path continues across the Río Pambre up into the hamlet of **Pontecampaña / Mato**

Pontecampaña

68km to Santiago | Altitude: 435m

Accommodation

Albergue Casa Domingo. Tel: (0034) 982 16 32 26
Beds: 14. Open May - Oct. Has dining & laundry facilties.

The camino now climbs up through oak woods along a stoney track. Continue on until you come to a road at which point turn left into **Casanova**

Casanova

67km to Santiago | Altitude: 485m

Accommodation

Albergue Municipal. Tel: (0034) 982 17 334 83
Beds: 20. Open all year. Has cooking & laundry facilties.

From Casanova continue on through the hamlets of **Campanilla** and then cross the border of the Province of Lugo and the Province of A Coruña into **Cornixa**. Follow the road until it turns off onto a path, which leads into **Leboreiro**

Leboreiro

64km to Santiago | Altitude: 450m

Information

Leboreiro's 13th century **Iglesia de Santa María** has an impressive stone carved tympanum depicting the Virgin and Child.

The **Casa de la Enfermería**, an

old pilgrim hospital donated by the Ulloa family, is opposite the church.

Accommodation

Albergue Municipal.
T: (0034) 981 50 73 51
Beds: 20. Open all year.

Cross the mediaeval bridge, which is dedicated to María Magdalena, over the Río Seco and into **Disecabo**.

The path now leads across a footbridge and along the outskirts of an industrial estate. Pass a fountain and rest area where the Knights & Dames of the Camino de Santiago have erected a monument. 1km later you arrive at the mediaeval Puente Velha where you cross over the Río Furelos into the village of **Furelos**

 # Furelos

Information

Here you will find the **Iglesia de San Juan,** which offers, guided tours, there is also a bar.

From Furelos it's a short walk along a street that runs alongside the main road. Turn right at the roundabout and then left onto the road leading into **Melide**

 # Melide

58km to Santiago | Altitude: 445m | Population: 7,800

Information

The *Camino Primitivo* joins up with the *Camino Frances* in Melide. King Alfonso IX found

Melide in the 13th century. The town's **Museo da Terra de Melide** is worth a visit if you fancy learning a bit more about the areas history.

The **Capilla de San Pedro & San Roque** dates from the time the town was founded and can be found on the Avenida de Lugo. Beside this you can see the 14th century stone **Cruceiro do Melide**, which is said to be the oldest in Galicia.

The 14th century **Iglesia de Sancti Spiritus,** in the Plaza del Convento, is built from stone from the old castle and was once a former Franciscan monastery. The 12th century **Iglesia de Santa Maria de Melide** can be found on the outskirts of the town and boasts a very impressive altar.

The **Iglesia del Carmen** can also be found on the outskirts of the town on the site of an old castle.

There are plenty of shops, bars and restaurant scattered around the narrow streets of the old town. You should also make a point of sampling some the specialty of Melide, *pulpo*.

Pulpo, octopus, is cooked in large copper pots, in it's own juice and sprinkled with paprika and served on wooden plates. Melide is reported to serve the best pulpo in all of Spain. **Pulpería Exequiel** on Avenido de Lugo is highly recommended.

Accommodation

Albergue Municipal,
Rúa San Antonio
T: (0034) 660 39 68 22
Beds: 130 in nine rooms. Open all year. Has cooking facilities.

Hostal Carlos *
Avenida de Lugo
T: (0034) 981 50 76 33

Hostal Estilo II *
Calle del Progreso
T: (0034) 50 51 53

Hostal Xaneiro I *
Rúa San Pedro 22
T: (0034) 981 50 50 15

Hostal Xaneiro II **
Avenida de la Habana 43
T: (0034) 981 50 61 40

After Melide the path winds its way up and down through forests, of oak, pine and eucalyptus trees. Continue on this path through **Raído** and **A Peroxa** then walk along a small stretch of road into **Boente**

Boente

52km to Santiago | Altitude: 385m

Accommodation

Os Albergue's Meson
T: (0034) 981 50 18 53
Beds: 10. Open Mar - Nov. Has dining facilties.

Leave the road onto a track that leads down into a valley before rising up on to a country road

into **Castañeda**

Castañeda

50km to Santiago | Altitude: 385m

Information

It was here that the pilgrims brought limestone from Triacastela, to the limekilns were the stone for The Cathedral in Santiago were finished. Today nothing remains of the kilns but you will find the **Iglesia de Santa María**

Accommodation
Casa Rural Milía *
T: (0034) 981 51 52 41

From here continue up along a

wooded hillside then down into a valley, following a quiet country road across the Río Iso into
Ribadiso do Baixo

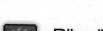

Ribadiso do Baixo

46km to Santiago | Altitude: 305m

Information

The small hamlet of Ribadiso do Baixo is in a beautiful location. The albergue is the restored **Hopistal de St Antón** and is one of the oldest pilgrim hospitals still in existence.

You'll find a bar and restaurant near to the albergue.

Accommodation

Albergue Municipal.
T: (0034) 981 50 11 85
Beds: 62. Open all year. Has cooking & laundry facilities.

Stage 31: Ribadiso do Baixo - O Pedrouzo
Map 6: Page 246 | Distance: 24.5km

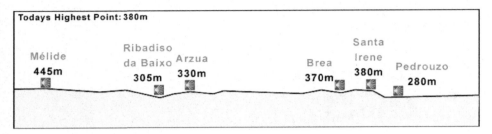

Todays Highest Point: 380m

Mélide 445m | Ribadiso da Baixo 305m | Arzua 330m | Brea 370m | Santa Irene 380m | Pedrouzo 280m

 ## Ribadiso do Baixo

46km to Santiago | Altitude: 305m

From Ribadiso follow the countryroad uphill through suburbs before reaching the town of **Arzúa**

Arzúa

43km to Santiago | Altitude: 330m | Population: 6,800

Information

Arzúa is the last major town before Santiago, with a population of around 7,000. It is famous for it's cheese, Quiexo, a smooth creamy cheese made with cow's milk and weighing around 1kg. The annual cheese festival, Fiesta de Quiexo, with over 100,000 varieties of cheese on display, is held on the first Sunday of March.

The main monuments of Arzúa include the 14th century **Capilla de la Magdalena** and the

modern 20th century **Igelsia de Santiago** with it's statue of Santiago Matamoro.

Accommodation

Albergue Municipal
Cimo do Lugar 6
T: (0034) 981 50 04 55
Beds: 46. Open all year. Has a cooking facility.

Albergue Don Quijote
Calle Lugo 130
T: (0034) 981 50 01 39
Beds: 50. Open all year. Has dining facilties.

Albergue Via Lactea
Calle José Antonio 26.
T: (0034) 981 50 05 81
Beds: 60. Open all year. Has cooking & laundry facilities as well as Internet access.

Albergue Ultreia
Calle Lugo 126
T: (0034) 981 50 04 71
Beds: 36. Open all year. Has cooking & laundry facilities as well as Internet access.

Albergue Santiago Apostal
Calle Calle Lugo 126
T: (0034) 981 50 04 71
Beds: 84. Open all year. Has cooking & laundry facilities.

Hostal Rúa *
Rúa de Lugo, 130
T: (0034) 981 50 01 39

Hotel Teodora **
Avenida de Lugo 38
T: (0034) 981 50 09 40

Hotel Suiza **
Carretera Santiago-Arzua.
T: (0034) 981 50 09 08
W: www.hsuiza.com

The Camino runs through the old part of Arzúa along the Calle del Carmen before crossing a stream into a wooded area.

The route passes through many small hamlets including **Raído**, **Cortobe**, then through **Calzada** into **Calle** where you'll find two cafés.

Continue on for another 1.5km through **Boavista** and **Alto** before reaching **Salceda** where there's a bar and a shop. After Salceda, pass a monument to pilgrim Guillermo Watt, who died here on route to Santiago, and cotinue on through **Xen** and **Ras** into **Brea**

 # Brea

28km to Santiago | Altitude: 370m

Accommodation

Albergue O Meson. Tel: (0034) 981 51 10 40
Beds: 10. Open all year. Has dining facilties. Also offers private rooms.

After Brea you have a choice to continue along the road into Santa Irene or to take a right along a path through a wooded area to **Alto de Santa Irene**. Here you'll find a fountain and a picnic / rest area. From here

cross the road onto a track that leads through woods, then a tunnel before arriving at **Santa Irene** with it's 18th century **Iglesia de Santa Irene**.

 # Santa Irene

24km to Santiago | Altitude: 380m

Accommodation

Albergue Municipal, on main road.
T: (0034) 660 39 68 25
Beds: 36. Open all year. Has cooking & laundry facilities.

Albergue Santa Irene
T: (0034) 660 39 68 25
Beds: 15. Open all year. Has cooking & laundry facilities.

Proceed on the camino along the road leading into **A Rúa**

A Rúa

22.5km to Santiago | Altitude: 275m

Accommodation

Casa Rural O Acivro *.
T: (0034) 981 51 13 16

Casa Rural Calvo *.
T: (0034) 981 81 44 01

Hotel O Pino * Rúa de Arca
T: (0034) 981 51 11 48

To reach O Pedrouza / Arca de Pino, continue through A Rúa along a small country road which leads to the main road (N-547).If you want to continue on to Santiago go straight ahead over the main road and back onto the track to **San Antón**. Else turn left here and after about 600m you'll come to **O Pedrouza / Arca de Pino**

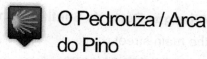

O Pedrouza / Arca do Pino

21.5km to Santiago | Altitude: 280m

Information

O Pedrouza / Arca do Pino has a lot of shops, bars and restaurants to choose from. Located not too far from your final destination of Santiago de Compostela.

The Pilgrim mass is held at 12:00 each day in Santiago Cathedral so to make it on time you may need to leave a little earlier than usual.

Accommodation

Albergue Municipal, beside the supermarket.
T: (0034) 660 39 68 26
Beds: 126. Open all year. Has cooking & laundry facilities.

Albergue Porta de Santiago, on the main street.

T: (0034) 981 51 11 03

Beds: 86. Open all year. Has Internet access.

Stage 32: O Pedrouzo - Santiago de Compostela
Map 6: Page 246 | Distance: 21.5km

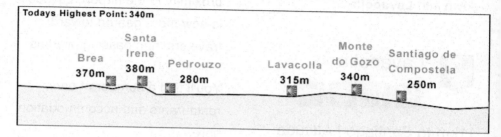

Todays Highest Point: 340m

Brea 370m | Santa Irene 380m | Pedrouzo 280m | Lavacolla 315m | Monte do Gozo 340m | Santiago de Compostela 250m

O Pedrouzo

21.5km to Santiago | Altitude: 280m

From O Pedrouzo / Arca do Pino take the track through eucalyptus forests and farmland through the village of San Antón and Amenal.

Continue uphill through Cimadevila and after a couple of kilometres you will come to a roundabout. From here turn left towards Santiago Airport and proceed along the track that runs along the end of the runway. Proceed past the airport and through **San Paio**

San Paio

14km to Santiago | Altitude: 300m

Casa Porta de Santiago *.
T: (0034) 902 88 97 61

Pass through San Paio and stay

on the country road uphill onto a tree-lined track that takes you down into **Lavacolla**

Lavacolla

🏨 🍴 ☕ 🛒

11km to Santiago | Altitude: 315m

Information

In mediaeval times, pilgrims used to wash themselves in the stream at Lavacolla before continuing their journey in Santiago.

According to the French monk Aymeric Picaud, who wrote the mediaeval pilgrim guide Codex Calixtinus, this was called Lavamentula, which translates into something like "Wash your privates". Due to its close proximity to the airport, Lavacolla is now more geared towards travelers than passing pilgrims.

You'll find a number of bars, restaurants and accommodation here.

Accommodation

Pensión San Paio *
Lugar de Lavacolla
T: (0034) 981 88 82 05

Hotel Garcas **
Calle Naval 2
T: (0034) 981 88 82 25
E:informacion@garcashotel.com
W: www.garcashotel.com

Hotel Pazo **Xan Xordo ****
T: (0034) 981 88 82 59
E: reservas@pazoxanxordo.com
W: www.pazoxanxordo.com

The camino nows runs past Lavacolla's parish church, **Iglesia de Benaval**. Just past the church and its fountain continue down to the river before climbing steeply uphill to **Vilamaior**

Vilamaior

10km to Santiago | Altitude: 360m

Casa Rural de Amancio *
T: (0034) 981 89 70 86

Continue through Vilamaior past the Television de Galicia Headquarters and turn left at the campsite opposite the Television de España building.

Proceed into **San Marcos** where you'll find a couple of bars and a café. In less than a kilometre from San Marcos you'll come to **Monte do Gozo**

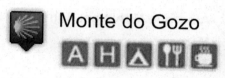

Monte do Gozo

5km to Santiago | Altitude: 340m

Information

Monte do Gozo, Mount of Joy, is where mediaeval pilgrims got their first view of the spires of Santiago cathedral. The suburbs block the view today.

A monument commemorating the visit of Pope John Paul II in the Holy Year of 1993 stands on top of the hill. A few hundred metres later you come to Albergue, which looks like a giant grey army barracks.

Although not a pretty sight, you are pretty much guaranteed a bed for the night if you decide to stay here. Within the complex are a number of shops, restaurants and bars.

Accommodation

Albergue Municipal San Marcos.
T: (0034) 981 55 89 42
Beds: 500 in twenty separate buildings. Open all year. Has cooking & laundry facilities. Also has a number of shops, restaurants and bars on site as well as campsite and private rooms.

After Monte do Gozote path goes across the motorway and a railway track before continuing past the Palacio de Congresos. On the other side of the road you'll find:

Albergue San Lázaro, Rúa de San Lázaro
T: (0034) 981 57 14 88
Beds: 80 in six rooms. Open all year. Has cooking & laundry facilities.

Continue along the main road past the Capilla de San Lázaro and take a left turn at Rúa do Valiño. On the left you'll find:

Albergue Acuario
Calle Estocolmo 2.
T: (0034) 981 57 54 38
Beds: 50. Open all year. Has dining & laundry facilities.

The path now goes straight along the Rúa das Fontinas, the Fonte dos Concheiros and across the roundabout onto Rúa dos Concheiros. Take a right onto Rúa de San Pedro and into the old town along Porta do Camiño. Walk down the Rúa Casas Reais onto the Rúa dos Animas and cross the Plaza de Cervaqntes onto Rúa da Acibechería.

Continue across the Praza da Immaculada, underneath the Arco del Abispo and into the Praza de Obradoiro to the front of the **Catedral de Santiago de Compostela**

Santiago de Compostela

🅰 🄷 ⛺ 🍴 ☕ € @ 🛒 ➕

0km to Santiago | Altitude: 250m | Population: 91,000

Information

According to legend, the remains of the apostle James were brought to Galicia and in the early 9th century they were discovered at Santiago de Compostela. The cathedral was built, on the spot where his remains were found, in his honour.

With it's twin Baroque towers standing high above the **Plaza del Obradoiro**, the cathedral is a beautiful sight, and in mediaeval times was the third most important place of pilgrimage after Jerusalem and Rome.

Around the Plaza del Obradoiro are a number of historic buildings including the elegant 18th century neoclassical **Pazo de Raxoi** built by Archbishop Raxoi in 1766, to house children who where either in the choir and / or from the workshop. It is now home to the city's Ayuntamiento. Also in the plaza is the 15th century **Hostal de los Reyes Católicos**, a pilgrim hostal founded by King Fernando & Queen Isabella. Today it is a parador hotel and regarded as one of the oldest hotels in the world.

The hotel provides free meals to pilgrims three times a day every day. Mealtimes are: breakfast at 09:00, lunch at 12:00 noon and dinner at 19:00. You must wait at the garage entrance to the left of the main hotel entrance and have a copy of your Compostella with you as proof you have completed the walk. In summer or peak times arrive early as the free meals are only limited to thefirst 10 pilgrims. You are entitled to take these meals within 3 days of your arrival in Santiago. To collect your certificate, Compostela, from the front of the Catedral take a right and walk up along the side of the cathedral onto Rúa de Gilmirez and take a right onto Rúa Vilar. Casa do Deán is on the right.

As long as you have completed at least the last 100km of the camino, you are eligible to receive the Compostela. The office is on the second floor and you will need to produce your pilgrim passport as proof you have completed the required 100km.

There is a travel desk on the ground floor, that offer discounts, if you need to make any return travel arrangements. A Pilgrim's Mass is held each day at noon for pilgrims in the Cathedral of Santiago de Compostela. Pilgrims who received the Compostela the day before have their countries of origin and the starting point of their pilgrimage announced at the Mass. The musical and visual highlight of

the mass is the synchronisation of the beautiful 'Hymn to Christ' with the spectacular swinging of the huge 'butafumeiro'. Other sites in the city include the Plaza de la Azabacheria, which originally opened the legendary

Puerta del Paradiso (door of the paradise), through which the pilgrims entered the cathedral. It was replaced by the neoclassical work of *Ventura Rodriguez*, which is still seen there today.

The impressive 16th century Baroque **Monasterio de San Martin Pinario** is situated in **Plaza de la Inmaculada** and was founded by a group of Benedictines who, shortly after the discovery of the Saint James' remains, settled in the place called Pignario, near the **Iglesia de Corticela** which now forms part of the Cathedral.

Legend has it that St. Francis of Assisi founded the **Convento de San Francisco de Valdediós** during his visit to Santiago de Compostela in 1214, at the place called Val de Dios. The land was purchased from the monks of San Mariño for the symbolic annual rent of a basket of trout.

St. Francis commissioned a coalman called Cotolay to build it, which he was able to do thanks to the miraculous discovery of a treasure.

Nothing is left of the original Gothic building except for five arches in the cloister and Cotolay's tomb. The Baroque monastery you see today was built in 17th century.

Accommodation

Albergue Seminario Menor de Belvis, Rúa Trompas.

T: (0034) 981 58 92 00
Beds: 177. Open all year. Has a
laundry facility as well as Internet
access.

Albergue San Lázaro

Rúa de San Lázaro.
T: (0034) 981 57 14 88
Beds: 80 in six rooms. Open all
year. Has cooking & laundry
facilities.

Albergue Acuario

Calle Estocolmo 2
T: (0034) 981 57 54 38
Beds: 50. Open all year. Has
dining & laundry facilities.

Hostal Estela *

Rúa Raxoi 1
T: (0034) 981 58 27 96

Hostal Barbantes *

Rúa do Franco 3.
T: (0034) 981 58 10 77

Camping As Cancela

Calle 25 de Xullo, 35
T: (0034) 981 58 02 66

Check:
http://tinyurl.com/hotels-santiago

Where to Eat

Most typical is Galician fish
including hake, turbot, grouper,
sea bass, sole, read bream and
monkfish that you will find in
abundance in Santiago's large
variety of restaurants.

Fish can be served grilled,
baked, or served in succulent
Galician-style stews with garlic
sauce, olive oil and a lot of
cayenne pepper in a **Caldeirada**,
a fish cocktail and in **Zarzuela**,
casserole which contains a
variety of spices, potatoes,
beans and prawns or clams.

Galicia 's many rivers also
provide a lot of salmon, trout and
lamprey. Another well-known
dish is **Empanada Gallega**, a
pie of fish, meat or vegetables.
Santiago de Compostela's
famous dessert is the so-called
Tarta de Santiago, whose
ingredients include a

combination of ground almond, eggs, sugar, butter and a little cinnamon topped by a layer of icing sugar bearing the Apostle's cross.

If dessert isn't your thing then there are many cheeses to choose from such as **Arzúa-Ulloa**, **O Cebreiro** or **San Simón,** a pointed, smoked cheese. By far the favourite Galician cheese is the **Queso de Tetilla**, characterised by its mild taste and distinctive conical shape.

To accompany your meal there are wines from all over Galicia to choose from. The wines of the region have a great reputation too, especially **Ribeiro**, young and fresh, but don't leave out the chance to try **Fefiñanes**, **Betanzos**, **Rosal**, **Valdeorras**, **Ulla** and **Amandi**.

Tourist Information/ Oficina de Turismo

Main Municipal Tourist Office, Rúa do Vilar, 63.
T: (0034) 981 55 51 29
Opening: Winter: every day 09:00-14:00 and 16:00-19:00. Easter and high season: every day 09:00-21:00.
E: info@santiagoturismo.com
W: www.santiagoturismo.com

Post Office / Oficina de Correos

Post Office. Travesía de Fonseca. General Information: Te (0034) 902 197 197.

Santiago Post Office:
T: (0034) 981 58 1 252.
Telegrams by Telephone:
T: (0034) 981 581 792.

Opening: Monday to Friday, 8.30 – 20.30. Saturday: 09.30 – 14:00.

Medical & Emergency Services

Emergency Number for all services: 112

Local Police: Pazo de Raxoi.
T: (0034) 981 54 23 23.
Emergencies: 092

National Police:
Rodrigo de Padrón 3.
T: (0034) 981 55 11 00.
Emergencies: 091

Accident & Emergency Ward,
Clinical Hospital. Vidán.
T: (0034) 981 95 00 00.

Others

Lost Property, Municipal Office
in Rúa da Trinidadee.
T: (0034) 981 54 30 27 / 981 54
23 23.

Train Station: Calle Hórreo.
T: (0034) 902 24 02 02 / 981 59
18 59

Bus Station: San Caetano 8.
T: (0034) 981 54 24 16
W: www.tussa.org

Airport: Lavacolla.
T: (0034) 981 54 75 00 / 981 54
75 01
W: www.aena.es

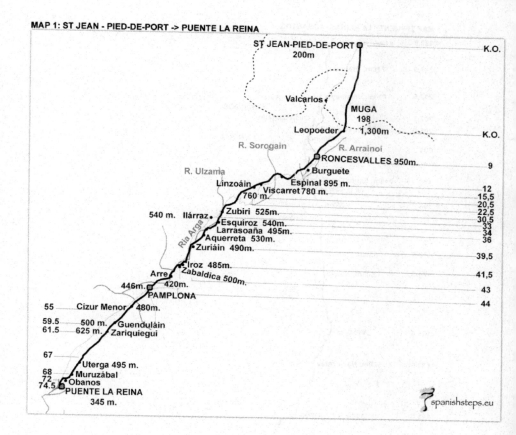

ST JEAN-PIED-DE-PORT
200m — K.O.

Valcarlos

MUGA
198
Leopoeder 1,300m — K.O.

R. Sorogain
R. Arrainoi
RONCESVALLES 950m. — 9
• Burguete
R. Ulzama
Linzoáin Espinal 895 m. — 12
760 m. Viscarret 780 m. — 15,5
— 20,5
540 m. Ilárraz • Zubiri 525m. — 22,5
Esquíroz 540m. — 30,5
Larrasoaña 495m. — 33
Aquerreta 530m. — 34
Zuriáin 490m. — 36
Ria Arga
Iroz 485m. — 39,5
Arre Zabaldica 500m. — 41,5
446m. 420m. — 43
PAMPLONA
— 44
55 Cizur Menor 480m.
59.5 500 m. Guenduláin
61.5 625 m. Zariquiegui

67
Uterga 495 m.
68 Muruzábal
72 Obanos
74.5 PUENTE LA REINA
345 m.

spanishsteps.eu

241

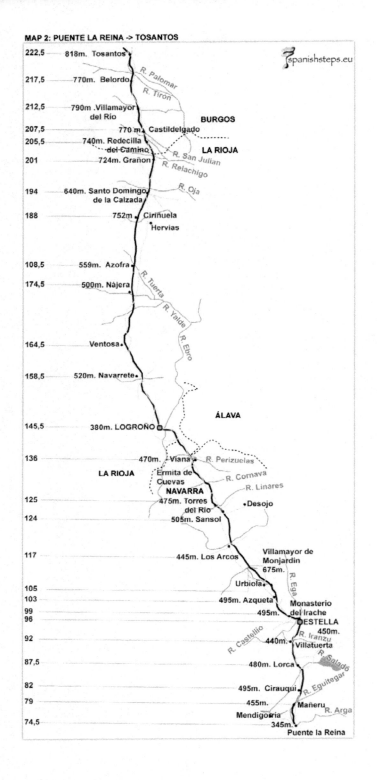

spanishsteps.eu

222,5 — 818m. Tosantos

R. Palomar

217,5 — 770m. Belordo

R. Tiron

212,5 — 790m. Villamayor
del Rio

BURGOS

207,5 — 770 m. Castildelgado

205,5 — 740m. Redecilla
del Camino

LA RIOJA

R. San Julian

201 — 724m. Grañon

R. Relachigo

194 — 640m. Santo Domingo
de la Calzada

R. Oja

188 — 752m. Ciriñuela

Hervias

108,5 — 559m. Azofra

174,5 — 500m. Nájera

R. Tuerta

R. Yalde

164,5 — Ventosa

R. Ebro

158,5 — 520m. Navarrete

ÁLAVA

145,5 — 380m. LOGROÑO

136 — 470m. Viana

R. Perizuelas

LA RIOJA

Ermita de
Cuevas

R. Cornava

NAVARRA

R. Linares

125 — 475m. Torres
del Rio

•Desojo

124 — 505m. Sansol

117 — 445m. Los Arcos

Villamayor de
Monjardin
675m.

R. Ega

105 — Urbiola

103 — 495m. Azqueta

Monasterio
del Irache

99 —
96 — 495m. ESTELLA

450m.

92 — 440m.

R. Iranzu

R. Castellio

Villatuerta

87,5 — 480m. Lorca

R. Salado

82 — 495m. Cirauqui

R. Eguitegar

79 — 455m.

Mañeru

R. Arga

Mendigorria

74,5 — 345m.

Puente la Reina

R. Carrión

CARRION DE LOS CONDES — 355
839m.

Villacázar de Sirga 809 m. R. Ucieza — 349

Virgen del Río

Revenga 793m. Villarmentero de Campos — 343,5
de Campos 788m. — 342
Poblacion de Villovieco
Campos 790m. — 338

Frómista 787m. — 333

PALENCIA

Boadilla
del Camino 784m. R. Canal de Castilla — 327,5

R. Berco

Itero BURGOS
de la Vega
769m. — 319

R. Odrilla

Castillo de
Matajudíos

Castrojeriz Ruinas de — 307
808m. San Anton — 304

R. Garganzuelo R. San Martín

Hontanas 867m. — 298
Olmillos
de Sassamón

R. Sambol

Hornillos R. Ormazuelas
del Camino
825m. Villanueva — 287
de Argaño

Rabé de
las Calzadas 840m. R. Urbel — 279
Tardajos 825m. — 277
Villabilla
de Burgos 880m. — 274

BURGOS
860m. — 268

Gamonal 870m. — 264

Villafria 880m. — 260
Orbaneja 925m. — 257
Cardeñuela 935m. — 255

Atapuerca
960m. — 249,5
Agés 970m. — 247

R. San Juan

San Juan
de Ortega 1000m. — 243,5

R. Oca

Valdefuentes — 237

La Pedraja Villafranca
Montes de Oca 950m. — 230,5
R. Palomar — 227
Espinosa del Camino 890m. — 224
Villambistia 870m.
Tosantos 818m. — 222,5

R. Pico

Autopista

R. Arlanzon

R. Vena

spanishsteps.eu

R. Tuerto

San Justo de laa Vega 847m. — 496
Crucero de Santo Toribio

A. Grillo

Santibañez de Valdeiglesias 845m. — 488
Villares 828m. — 485,5

R. Órbigo   Hospital de Órbigo
819m. — 483

R. Huerga   870m. — 476
San Martín del Camino

R. Lavadero   890m. — 471,5
R. Raposeras

Villadangos del Paramo
A. del Valle   San Miguel del Camino 905m. — 464
Valverde de la Virgen 890m. — 462,5
Autopista

La Virgen del Camino 905m. — 459
A. Oncina   Trabajo del Camino 835m. — 455

R. Esla   LEÓN 838m. — 451,5
R. Bernesga

R. Torio

Railway   Valdelafuente 860m. — 439
Arcahueja   850m. — 443,5
R. Porma

Villarente 805m. — 439
Villamoros 800m. — 438

Mansilla de las Mulas 795m. — 432
A. Grande   R. Moro

Villamarco.
N 601   Reliegos 820m. — 426
A. Valdeviñas

R. Esla
A. Valdearcos
A. Buen Solana   A. Utielga
A. Valdeasneros

El Burgo Ranero 875m. — 413,5

A. Majuelos
Bercianos del 850m   Calzadilla de los Hermanillo 885m.
Real Camino   R. Coso — 406

R. Cea

R. Calzada   Calzada del Coto 820m. — 400,5

R. Valderaduey   Sahagún de Campos 816m. — 395,5

R. Sequillo   San Nicolás del Real Camino 840m. — 387,5
A. Templarios   LEÓN
Moratinos 860m. — 385

Terradillos de Templarios 885m. — 381,5
Ledigos 880m.   PALENCIA — 379
Santa María de las Tiendas
R. Cueza   Calzadilla de la Cueza 860m. — 372
A. Valdealmienzo

A. Pozo Amargo   Bustillo del Páramo

R. Carrion

CARRÍON DE LOS CONDES 839m. — 355

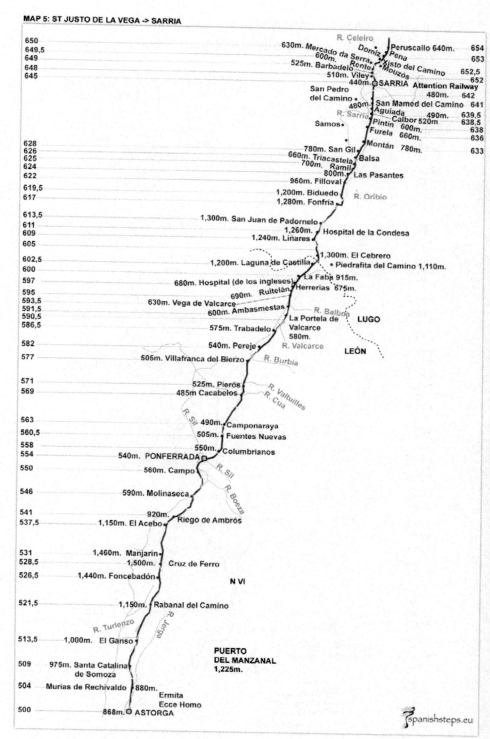

761 — **SANTIAGO DE COMPOSTELA 260m**
Autopista — R. Sal

756 — 340m. San Marcos — Capilla de San
752,5 — 340m. Villamayor — Marcos 350m.
751 — 300m. Lavacolla
R. Lavacolla — San Payo
745 — 240m. Amenal — 320m. 749
743 — 280m. San Anton
741 — 300m. Rua — Burgo
739 — 380m. Santa Irene — 320m. 742
738 — 400m. Cerceda
737 — 380m. Brea
733 — 360m. Salceda
S. Verisimo — Boavista
730 — 340m. Ferreiros — 360m. 732
R. Langüello
728 — 380m. Calzada
725 — 360m. Raldo
723,5 — Cortobe 400m.
722,5 — 390m. Arzua
R. Iso
720 — 300m. Ribadiso
716,5 — 415m. A. Ribeiral
714 — 400m. Boente — Castañeda
713,5 — 440m. Peroja — R. Boente
711,5 — 430m. Raído
708,5 — 455m. Mellid
707 — 415m. Furelos — LA CORUÑA
R. Furelos
703 — 440m. Leboreiro
702 — 460m. Campanilla — A. Seco
699,5 — 480m. Casanova — Porto de Bois 420m.
Pontecampana 420m. — 698
697 — 480m. San Julián del Camino
R. Pambre
Palas de Rey — R. Ruxián
690,5 — Lamelas 565m. — 693
Brea — LUGO
688,5 — 600m. Lestedo — 690
685 — 580m. Ligonde — Portos 580m. — 687,5
684 — 640m. Lameiros
R. Portos
679,5 — 680m. Prebisa 660m. — 683
677 — 600m. Castromayor — R. Ligonde
Ventas de Narón 700m.
675,5 — 540m. Gonzar — Hospital — 681
672,5 — 500m. Tojibó — Guntin
R. Torres
663,5 — 480m.
659 — Couto — Portomarín 350m. — 667
661 — 580m. Moimentos — Vilacha 440m.
655 — Mercadoiro — 665
654 — Parrocha
Lavandeira 640m. — Rozas — 659,5
652,5 — Xisto del Camino
652 — Mirallos 650m. — 658
Brea — 656
650 — 630m. — Peruscallo
649,5 — 600m. Rente — Mouzos
649 — 525m. Barbadelo — Mercado da Serra
648 — 510m. Viley
645 — 440m. SARRIA

7spanishsteps.eu

Useful Links

Below are some useful links to help you find all you need to make your Camino the best it can possibly be. Links have been shortened for your convenience.

Spanish Steps Amazon Store

http://tinyurl.com/camino-amazon-store

Walking Equipment

http://tinyurl.com/camino-gear

http://tinyurl.com/camino-footwear

http://tinyurl.com/camino-cameras

http://tinyurl.com/camino-journal

Accommodation

http://tinyurl.com/camino-hotels

http://tinyurl.com/camino-budget-hotels

http://tinyurl.com/hotels-pamplona

http://tinyurl.com/hotels-burgos

http://tinyurl.com/hotels-santiago

Travel Insurance

http://tinyurl.com/camino-insurance

Book A Flight

http://tinyurl.com/camino-flights

Car Hire

http://tinyurl.com/camino-cars

Learn Spanish

http://tinyurl.com/camino-spanish

Santiago: The Cuckoo and the Pilgrim

This book will transport you with Joe and his walking companions along the Camino de Santiago through the vineyards and sunflower fields of southern France, over the Pyrenees by the Pass of Ibaneta, through the wheat plains of the Spanish meseta and into the mountains of Galicia to the Shrine of St James in the city of Santiago.

Check: http://tinyurl.com/cuckoo-and-the-pilgrim

Notes

Notes

CPSIA information can be obtained
at www.ICGtesting.com
Printed in the USA
LVOW01s1019120317
526915LV00008B/753/P